BIG
IDEAS
OF SCIENCE
REFERENCE LIBRARY

PEARSON

Boston, Massachusetts
Chandler, Arizona
Glenview, Illinois
Upper Saddle River, New Jersey

ISBN-13: 978-0-13-369873-2
ISBN-10: 0-13-369873-4

1 2 3 4 5 6 7 8 9 10   V057   14 13 12 11 10

CONTENTS

KEY
These symbols appear in the top right corner below the topic name
to connect the topic to the branches of science.

 Earth Science   Life Science   Physical Science

BIG IDEAS OF EARTH SCIENCE 🌍

The Big Ideas of earth science help us understand our changing planet, its long history, and its place in the universe. Earth scientists study Earth and the forces that change its surface and interior.

Earth is part of a system of objects that orbit the sun.

Asteroids
Astronomy Myths
Bay of Fundy
Comets
Constellations
Earth
Gravity
Jupiter's Moons
Mars
Mars Rover
Mercury
Meteorites
Moon
Neptune
Pluto
Saturn
Solar Eclipse
Solar Power
Space Probes
Summer Solstice
Uranus
Venus

Earth is 4.6 billion years old and the rock record contains its history.

Atmosphere
Dating Rocks
Deep Sea Vents
Dinosaurs
Eryops
Extinction
Family Tree
Fossils
Geologic Time
Giant Mammals
Ice Age

Earth's land, water, air, and life form a system.

Altitude
Atacama Desert
Atmosphere
Aurora Borealis
Buoys
Doppler Radar
Dust Storms
Earth's Core
Floods
Fog
Gliding
Predicting Hurricanes
Rainbows
Sailing
Snowmaking
Storm Chasing
Thunderstorms
Weather Fronts

Earth is the water planet.

Amazon River
Beaches
Drinking Water
Everglades
Great Lakes
Mid-Ocean Ridge
Niagara Falls
Ocean Currents
Sea Stacks
Surfing
Thermal Imaging
Tsunami
Upwelling
Water

Earth is a continually changing planet.

Acid Rain
Afar Triangle
Caves
Coal

Colorado Plateau
Colorado River
Coral Reefs
Crystals
Dunes
Earthquakes
Equator
Fluorescent Minerals
Geocaching
Geodes
Geysers
Glaciers
Gold Mining
Hoodoos
Ice Age
Islands
Kilauea
Landslides
Lava
Mapping
Marble Quarries
Mid-Ocean Ridge
Mount Everest
Niagara Falls
Rain Forest
Rubies
Sea Stacks
Soil
Terrace Farming
Tour de France
Tsunami

Human activities can change Earth's land, water, air, and life.

Air Pollution
Energy Conservation
Equator
Fuel Cell Cars
Global Warming
Ice Age
Ocean Currents
Rain Forest
Shelter

The universe is very old, very large, and constantly changing.

Big Bang Theory
Black Holes
Constellations
Hubble Space Telescope
Milky Way
Quasars
Universe

Science, technology, and society affect each other.

Astronauts
Hubble Space Telescope
Jetpacks
International Space
    Station
Mars Rover
Predicting Hurricanes
Robots
Satellite Dish
Science at Work
Space Technology
Space Tourism
Virtual World

Scientists use mathematics in many ways.

Buoys
Doppler Radar
Mars Rover
Measurement
Neptune

Scientists use scientific inquiry to explain the natural world.

Extinction
Predicting Hurricanes
Wind Power
Neptune

BIG IDEAS OF LIFE SCIENCE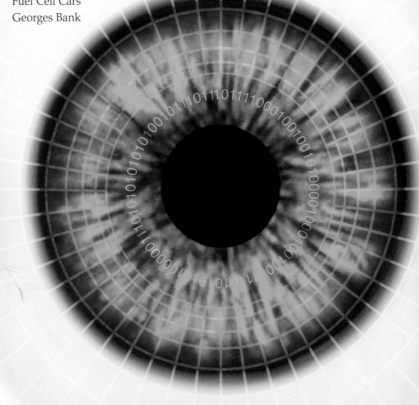

Life scientists study organisms, their life processes, and how they interact with one another and their environment. The Big Ideas of life science help us understand how living things are organized, how they get and use energy, and how they reproduce.

Living things grow, change, and reproduce during their lifetimes.

Animal Communication
Bush Baby
Courtship Rituals
Echolocation
Gorillas
Hummingbirds
Hypothalamus
Instinct
Marsupials
Menstrual Cycle
Penguins
Pregnancy
Puberty
Sea Horse
Seals
Sleep
Sloth
Tasmanian Devil
Twins
Worms

Living things are made of cells.

Blood Types
Cactus
Cell Division
Microscopes
Quarks and Leptons
Scent Pollution
Skeletons

Living things are alike yet different.

Adaptations
Aerogels
Bacteria
Bats
Bears
Cactus
Common Cold
DNA Connections
Exoskeleton
Family Tree
Farming
Ferns
Flowers
Frankenfoods
Fungi
Geckos
Giant Mammals
Gila Monster
Insects
Jellyfish
Naming
Patterns in Nature
Plant Tricks
Rain Forest
Red Tide
Redwoods
Scent Pollution
Skeletons
Snakes
Soil
Spiders
Survival
Symmetry
Taco Science
Whales

Living things interact with their environment.

Acid Rain
Air Pollution
Amazon River
Atacama Desert
Bats
Bay of Fundy
Beaches
Biodiversity
Biofuels
Bush Baby
Butterflies
Camouflage
Coal
Colorado Plateau
Deep Sea Vents
Energy Conservation
Everglades
Farming
Forestry
Frozen Zoo
Fuel Cell Cars
Georges Bank

Global Warming
GPS Tracking
Great Lakes
Hybrid Vehicles
Insects
Islands
Kilauea
Light Bulbs
Mid-Ocean Ridge
Mount Everest
Oil Spills
Patterns in Nature
Plant Invasion
Plastic
Population Growth
Rain Forest
Recycling
Red Tide
Renewal
Sea Horse
Seaweed
Seed Bank
Sharks
Shelter
Skywalk

Sloth
Soil
Solar Power
Supercooling Frogs
Sushi
Upwelling
Vultures

Genetic information passes from parents to offspring.

Blood Types
Colorblindness
DNA Evidence
Frankenfoods
Frozen Zoo
Genetic Disorders
Human Genome Project
Hummingbirds
Mutations
Probability

Living things get and use energy.

Algae
Barracuda
Birds
Cell Division
Elephants
Hummingbirds
New Body Parts
Octopus
Scorpion
Sea Horse
Seals
Sour Milk
Tasmanian Devil
Teeth

Structures in living things are related to their functions.

ACL Tear
Aerobic Exercise
ALS
Altitude
Animal Bodies
Birds
Blood Pressure
Blood Types
Brain Power
Broken Bones
Defibrillators
Digestion
Dolphins
Drinking Water
Exoskeleton
Fats

Gliding
Hearing Loss
Heartbeat
Hummingbirds
Jellyfish
Kidney Transplant
Laser Eye Surgery
Left vs. Right Brain
Marsupials
No Smoking
Open-Heart Surgery
Prosthetic Limb
Scent Pollution
Sea Turtles
Simulators
Singing
Skeletons
Skin
Sleep
Sloth
Steroids
Superfoods
Teeth
The Bends
Tour de France
Tweeters and Woofers
Vitamins and Minerals
Weightlifting

Living things change over time.

DNA Connections
Family Tree
Gorillas
Islands
Madagascar
Racehorses

Living things maintain constant conditions inside their bodies.

Allergies
Astronauts
Cancer Treatment
Common Cold
HIV/AIDS
Malaria
Marathon Training
Mold
MRI
Pandemic
Rats
Rheumatoid Arthritis
Scent Pollution
Sleep
Thermal Imaging
Vaccines
Working Body

Scientists use mathematics in many ways.

Census
Estimation
Hazardous Materials
Measurement
Probability
Simulators

Science, technology, and society affect each other.

Biomimetics
Clinical Trials
DNA Evidence
Eye Scan
Human Genome Project
Prosthetic Limb
Robots
Science at Work
Truth in Advertising

Scientists use scientific inquiry to explain the natural world.

BPA
Crittercam
Forensics
Human Genome Project
Naming
Quarks and Leptons
Truth in Advertising

BIG IDEAS OF PHYSICAL SCIENCE

Physical scientists study matter and energy. The Big Ideas of physical science help us describe the objects we see around us and understand their properties, motions, and interactions.

A net force causes an object's motion to change.

Asteroids
Astronauts
Bridges
Collision
Crew
Drag Racing
Formula 1 Car
Gravitron
Gravity
Hockey
Hovercraft
Jetpacks
Meteorites
Quasars
Roller Coaster
Sailing
Skydiving
Snowboard
Tour de France

Energy can take different forms but is always conserved.

Aerogels
ALS
Aurora Borealis
Bicycles
Black Holes
Bridges
Bungee Jumping
Catapults
Cordless Drill
Crew
Defibrillators
Earth's Core
Energy Conservation
Geocaching
Gliding
Headphones
Hoover Dam
Hybrid Vehicles
Lichtenberg Figures
Lifting Electromagnets
Light Bulbs
Microscopes
MP3 Player
MRI
Niagara Falls
Radio
Roller Coaster
Rube Goldberg Devices
Skyscraper
Skywalk
Submarines
Taco Science
Thermal Imaging
Weightlifting

Waves transmit energy.

Animal Communication
Cellphone
Color
Digital Camera
Doppler Radar
Echolocation
Eye Scan
Fluorescent Minerals
Geocaching
GPS Tracking
Guitar
Headphones
Hearing Loss
Holograms
Hubble Space Telescope
Hummingbirds
Laser Eye Surgery
Lighthouse
Microscopes
Mirages
Night Vision Goggles
Predicting Hurricanes
Radio
Rainbows
Rubies
Satellite Dish
Sea Stacks
Seaweed
Singing
Solar Power
Sonic Booms
Surfing
Thunderstorms
Tsunami
Tweeters and Woofers
Virtual World

Atoms are the building blocks of matter.

Acid Rain
Black Holes
Body Protection
Caves
Creating Elements
Crystals
Geckos
Glass
Gold Mining
Mars Rover
Melting Point
Meteorites
Nuclear Medicine
Prosthetic Limb
Quarks and Leptons
Steel
The Bends
Water

Mass and energy are conserved during physical and chemical changes.

Digestion
Earth
Fire Extinguishers
Fireworks
Forestry
Hovercraft
Ice Houses
  Lava
    Melting Point
      Scent Pollution
      Snowmaking
        Supercooling
          Frogs
          The Bends

Scientists use mathematics in many ways.

Buoys
Hazardous Materials
Mars Rover
Measurement
Wind Tunnel

Scientists use scientific inquiry to explain the natural world.

Biomimetics
Forensics
Quarks and Leptons
Wind Power

Science, technology, and society affect each other.

Bridges
Cellphone
Formula 1 Car
Hubble Space
  Telescope
Light Bulbs
Prosthetic Limb
Robots
Science at Work

SNOWBOARD

You are at the top of the slope. As you glide downhill, you move faster and faster. You lean one way and then the other, twisting and turning to put gentle pressure here and a slight shift of weight there. As smooth as it looks, snowboarding involves tricky moves that use a lot of skill and agility—and physics. A snowboard slides on a thin film of water. The surface of the snow under the board melts because friction between the board and snow produces heat. The water lubricates the bottom of the board, reducing the friction. The force of gravity pulls the board and rider down the hill. At the same time, friction opposes the motion and allows the boarder to vary the speed and direction. When snowboarders participate in different types of competitive events, each rider chooses a board and riding technique that will generate the right amount of friction to control the snowboard.

Boarders use helmets to absorb and distribute force in a fall.

Bending the knees helps keep the center of gravity above the part of the board that is touching the snow.

SLALOM ▼

On a slalom course, the racer has to zigzag between sets of poles, called *gates*, by making precise turns while trying to maintain the highest possible speed. One way to reduce friction between the snow and the board is to reduce the contact area between the surfaces. Racers do this by leaning their weight over one of the long edges of the board, so only the edge is in contact with the snow.

SNOWBOARD CROSS ▶

In the snowboard cross, several racers—usually four—rush down the slope at the same time. They compete both for speed and position on the course. The course challenges them with jumps, bumps, sharp turns, and obstacles. Courses are often narrow, so racers sometimes bump into each other. Racers typically wear more padding for this event than for other types of racing. While the boards used in a slalom race, called *alpine boards*, are ridden in just one direction, the freestyle boards used in the cross are curved at both ends, allowing the rider to switch stance, pointing either end downhill.

did you know?

....

THE FIRST SNOWBOARD ON THE MARKET WAS THE SNURFER™, INVENTED BY SHERMAN POPPEN IN 1965 WHEN HE FASTENED TWO SKIS TOGETHER TO MAKE A "SNOW SURFBOARD" FOR HIS DAUGHTER.

Half-pipe boards are shorter and springier than other boards, resulting in lower speeds but better aerial tricks.

AIR ABOVE THE HALF PIPE ▲

Half-pipe boarders win with technique and creativity. The competition takes place in a half-cylinder-shaped course dug deep into a hill. The course runs down the slope. Riders start by gaining speed going down one side of the cylinder and then use the energy they gain to come up over the rim of the pipe and perform acrobatic aerial tricks. Each time a rider reaches a rim, he or she keeps moving up into the air. Riders spin and flip in the air, land back in the half pipe, and speed over to the opposite rim for the next trick.

Snowboard cross racers can reach speeds of more than 55 miles per hour (almost 89 km/h).

When the edge of the board pushes against the snow, the snow pushes back, changing the board's direction.

SNOW MAKING

Have you ever planned a day of skiing or snowboarding, only to cancel the trip because there isn't enough snow on the slopes? What a disappointment! Fortunately, most ski resorts can make snow. Snow guns are machines that create a fine mist of water and then blast the mist into the air. As the mist cools and falls back toward the ground, the droplets freeze into snow. Smaller drops that fall farther are needed when the air temperature is warmer. In colder temperatures, larger drops and shorter distances can be used. Snow makers may also use a nucleating agent—usually a harmless bacterium that triggers the freezing process. Water molecules surround the bacterium and can freeze at warmer temperatures than they would otherwise. To use snow-making machines, ski resorts must install water pipes up the side of a mountain. They also need pumps and an air compressor or a large fan.

Computer systems automatically adjust the amount of water and air a machine uses based on outdoor temperature, humidity, and wind.

NATURAL SNOWFALL ▶
Natural snow comes from water vapor in the atmosphere. Clouds form when this water vapor condenses. When the droplets in the clouds get too heavy, they fall to the ground. If it is cold enough, the droplets form tiny ice crystals. Pure water freezes at temperatures lower than 32°F (0°C), but most water is not pure. Particles such as dust and bacteria are found in water vapor. Water condenses around the particle, which becomes the nucleus, or center, of the ice crystal. Several ice crystals form a snowflake.

did you know?...............................
ALMOST ALL COMPETITIVE SKI EVENTS TAKE PLACE ON SNOW MADE BY SNOW MACHINES.

A fan gun with hundreds of nozzles sprays a fine mist of water over a stream of air.

▲ BLASTING MAN-MADE SNOW

Snow guns draw water from a nearby pond, river, reservoir, or other source and pump the water into the machine. Some snow guns use compressed air to blast the water into a mist and into the atmosphere. Other snow guns use a nozzle similar to a spray bottle nozzle to atomize the water into a fine spray. A high-speed fan blows this mist into the air.

Some snow guns must be positioned at higher elevations to ensure that water droplets will freeze before hitting the ground.

Hoses for both water and compressed air feed the snow gun.

SOIL

Healthy soil is the foundation of land ecosystems. Soil begins when rock is weathered into smaller grains, or sediments, and minerals such as sand, clay, and salt. Minerals and sediments, however, are just one part of soil. Another part is called *humus*. Humus is a dark-colored substance that is created when organisms such as bacteria, fungi, and other decomposers break down dead plant and animal materials. Water and air are also found in soil. Different plants need different mixes of sediment and nutrients. Fortunately, there are thousands of soil types. The type of soil that develops in a particular area depends on rock type, climate, local organisms, how steep or level the land is, and time. Fertile soils have plentiful humus and nutrients to support new plant growth.

MUTUAL SUPPORT ▶

Plants and soil support each other. Soil gives plants a place to grow, and provides water and nutrients. Plants, in turn, support the soil—the roots keep the soil from being eroded by wind or water. Dead plant matter decomposes, enriching the soil with humus.

▼ LIVING SOIL

Rich soil teems with microscopic bacteria and fungi. Tiny organisms such as nematodes and mites are easy to overlook, but they far outnumber the more familiar—and more visible—worms and insects. Rabbits may be one of the most noticeable organisms living in soil, but they are among the least common.

did you know? A CUP OF SOIL CONTAINS AS MANY BACTERIA AS THERE ARE PEOPLE ON EARTH. ....

The topsoil, also called the *A-horizon*, supports most plant life, including the grass these rabbits enjoy.

As the rabbits burrow, they mix materials in the subsoil, also called the *B-horizon*, and create paths for rainwater and air to enter.

Plants use nitrogen from the soil to make chlorophyll, the green pigment that captures energy for photosynthesis.

Plant roots absorb mineral water—a solution of essential trace minerals and other compounds found in soil.

▲ NEW SOIL FROM SCRAPS

Heavy equipment turns over compost at a commercial facility, but it is bacteria, fungi, and worms that do the heavy lifting. These decomposers change grass trimmings, food scraps, and other organic matter into a nutrient-rich material similar to humus. Commercial compost is sold to farmers, landscapers, and others who use it to replenish soil naturally.

This tree root, though dead, still holds soil in place. As it rots, it will enrich the soil.

SOLAR ECLIPSE

Have you ever observed a solar eclipse? A solar eclipse occurs when the moon passes in front of the sun and casts a shadow on Earth. Imagine the sky getting dark on an otherwise sunny afternoon. For several minutes, it is dark enough to see some of the brightest stars and planets shining in the sky. Moments later, the sky begins to brighten. Within the next hour, it is broad daylight again, as if the brief period of darkness never happened. Because the sun's rays can damage your eyes, you cannot safely view a solar eclipse without specially designed eye protection. With this protection, you can see the dark disk of the moon slowly move in front of the sun, sometimes completely covering it. After several minutes, you can see the moon slowly move past the sun.

▼ THE MOON'S PATH

Several factors determine how long an eclipse will take. The orbits of the moon and Earth and their distances from both each other and the sun are key. Partial phases, during which the moon gradually covers and uncovers the sun, can each take about an hour. A total eclipse can last up to about 7 minutes. This image combines many photos of the stages of the eclipse into one photo. It shows the path of the moon as it passes in front of the sun, as seen from Zambia in Southern Africa.

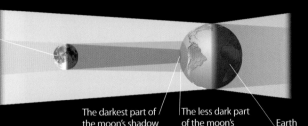

The sun illuminates the side of the moon that we cannot see.

The darkest part of the moon's shadow is called the *umbra*. Where the umbra falls, a total eclipse is visible from Earth.

The less dark part of the moon's shadow is called the *penumbra*. Where the penumbra falls, a partial eclipse is visible from Earth.

Earth

◀ AN ECLIPSE IS POSSIBLE WHEN . . .

A solar eclipse can happen only during the new moon phase, when the moon passes between the sun and Earth and the three are in near-perfect alignment. We don't usually see a solar eclipse, because the moon's path is generally above or below the position of the sun. For a solar eclipse to occur, the moon's path must cross directly in front of the sun.

did you know?..

THE NEXT TOTAL SOLAR ECLIPSE THAT WILL BE VISIBLE FROM THE UNITED STATES WILL TAKE PLACE ON AUGUST 21, 2017.

◀ SHOWTIME

Normally the corona—the sun's extended outer atmosphere—is not visible, because the sun's surface, or photosphere, is so bright. The corona can be seen only during a total eclipse, when the moon covers the sun completely. The corona glows around the edges of the moon and can reach temperatures of up to 3.5 million degrees Fahrenheit (2 million degrees Celsius).

The corona extends more than 621,370 miles (1 million km) from the sun's surface. The solar wind originates here.

During a total solar eclipse, prominences—arcs of flaming gases erupting from the sun's surface—can be seen flaring out from behind the moon.

▲ THE PATH OF TOTALITY

Total solar eclipses happen once every year and a half, but the chances of seeing one are slim. The umbra moves across Earth's surface. Its path, called the *path of totality*, is about 167 miles (269 km) in diameter. The shadow travels at about 1,242 miles (2,000 km) per hour—and often crosses the ocean and remote places.

SOLAR POWER

A stove, a computer, a TV, and a car all require energy to run. And at least some of this energy probably comes from burning fossil fuels. Coal, oil, and natural gas are the three most common fossil fuels. Fossil fuels are energy-rich substances, but they are in limited supply. Solar power, on the other hand, is renewable, or in constant supply, and it does not pollute the environment. Today, you can find solar-powered gadgets like flashlights, watches, and computer mice. Solar power is being used to provide electricity and hot water to homes and to pump water from wells. And solar power is being used to run golf carts and to provide power for fans or other devices in automobiles.

▼ SOLAR THERMAL POWER

These are just some of the 624 mirrors that belong to the PS10 solar thermal power plant in Sanlúcar la Mayor, Spain. Each mirror, called a *heliostat*, reflects the sun's rays toward a receiver at the top of a concrete tower 377 feet (115 m) tall. The heat from the rays changes water into steam, which is used to turn electricity-producing turbines. A second, newer plant, using 1,255 heliostats and a tower 525 feet (160 m) tall, produces 20 megawatts of power, almost double that of the PS10.

did you know? YOU CAN MAKE A SOLAR OVEN WITH A PIZZA BOX, BLACK PAPER, ALUMINUM FOIL, AND PLASTIC.

As the sun moves across the sky, each mirror turns to reflect the sun's rays toward the central tower.

Each mirror is about as tall as a 3-story building.

▲ PORTABLE POWER

This solar-powered battery charger can charge your cellphone and other portable devices. It uses solar cells, also called *photovoltaic cells*, to convert solar energy into electricity.

SOLAR COOKING ▶

A woman in Nepal uses a solar oven to boil the water in her teakettle. The curved surface of the oven reflects the sun's rays to one point in the oven. A kettle or other cooking utensil placed at this point is heated by the converging rays. No other source of energy is required, and no smoke from burning fuel enters the air.

SONIC BOOMS

A jet plane speeds across the sky overhead and a sound like thunder follows. Boom! Was that the roar of its engines? Actually, it was a sonic boom. A sonic boom occurs whenever an object, such as the plane, travels faster than the speed of sound. To understand why a sonic boom occurs, think about sound as the movement of air molecules. When the plane moves through the air, it pushes the air molecules, producing pressure waves. These waves are alternating high pressure and low pressure areas of air. As the plane flies through the air, these waves travel in all directions including to the ground. You hear each wave as normal airplane noise. When the plane travels faster than the speed of sound, the waves produced by the plane can travel only as fast as the speed of sound, which is slower than the plane. Because of this, the waves "run into" each other and bunch up, forming very large waves, called *shock waves*. A shock wave is actually a sudden increase in pressure. When the shock waves reach your eardrum, you hear a sonic boom. The sudden increase in pressure has the same effect as the sudden expansion of air produced by an explosion. People nearby hear the sonic boom of the explosion when the shock wave passes them.

did you know? THE CRACK OF A WHIP IS A TINY SONIC BOOM CAUSED BY THE SPEED OF THE TIP TRAVELING FASTER THAN THE SPEED OF SOUND.

Vapor cone or condensation cloud

◄ VAPOR CONE

When a plane or rocket travels near the speed of sound, a cone-shaped cloud, called a *vapor cone*, may form around the object. This cloud forms due to a sudden acceleration of the airplane at high speeds, causing an abrupt drop in pressure of the air passing over the plane. When the air pressure decreases, the air temperature also decreases and water vapor in the air condenses into tiny droplets of water. Because this can happen to an object traveling just below the speed of sound, a sonic boom may not be heard.

FASTER THAN THE SPEED OF SOUND

On October 14, 1947, Chuck Yeager, a test pilot with the United States Air Force, reached a speed of 700 miles per hour (about 1,126 km/h) or 1.06 times the speed of sound (also known as Mach 1.06). Yeager was flying a rocket-powered X-1 research plane. This plane, 31 feet (about 9.4 m) long with a wingspan of 28 feet (about 8.5 m), was modeled after the shape of a .50-inch (1.27-cm) bullet. With this feat, Yeager became the first person to travel faster than the speed of sound. To calculate an object's Mach number, you compare its speed with the speed of sound at the same temperature. For example, the speed of sound in air at Yeager's flying altitude of 40,000 feet (12,192 m) is about 660 miles per hour (1,062 km/h). When you divide Yeager's speed by the speed of sound—700/660 (1,126/1,062)—you get Mach 1.06.

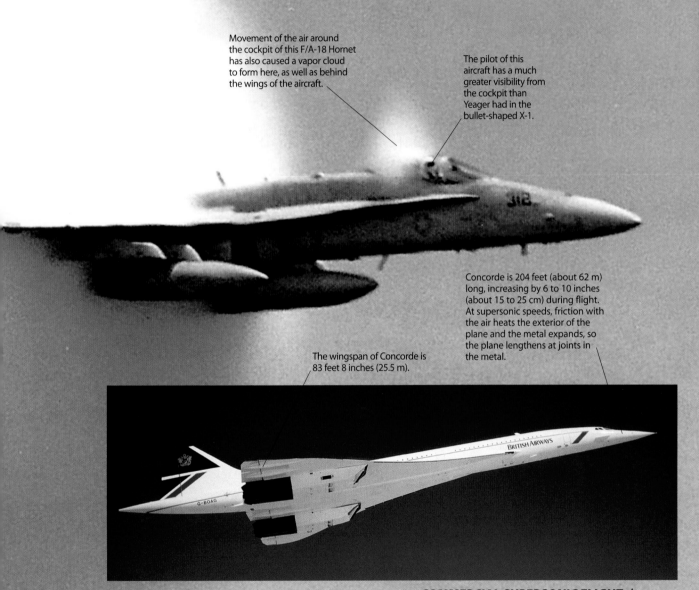

Movement of the air around the cockpit of this F/A-18 Hornet has also caused a vapor cloud to form here, as well as behind the wings of the aircraft.

The pilot of this aircraft has a much greater visibility from the cockpit than Yeager had in the bullet-shaped X-1.

Concorde is 204 feet (about 62 m) long, increasing by 6 to 10 inches (about 15 to 25 cm) during flight. At supersonic speeds, friction with the air heats the exterior of the plane and the metal expands, so the plane lengthens at joints in the metal.

The wingspan of Concorde is 83 feet 8 inches (25.5 m).

COMMERCIAL SUPERSONIC FLIGHT ▲

Flight that is faster than the speed of sound, called *supersonic flight*, is not just for the military. Fourteen Concordes®, supersonic commercial aircraft, carried more than 2.5 million people, starting in 1976 and ending in 2003. Concorde could fly as fast as 1,350 miles per hour (almost 2,173 km/h), traveling from London to New York in only 3.5 hours—half the time needed by standard aircraft.

A display showed Concorde passengers their speed and altitude while in flight. Mach 2 means that the plane is moving at twice the speed of sound. At an altitude of 54,000 feet (16,459 m), the speed of sound is about 660 miles per hour (1,062 km/h). That means the Concorde is flying at 1,320 miles per hour (2,124 km/h).

MACH 2.00 FEET 54000

SOUR MILK

Long ago, someone who accidentally had left an open pail of milk standing for too long might have noticed that the milk had begun to thicken, and figured the milk was ruined. But then people discovered that the thickened milk lasted longer than fresh milk and had a pleasant, sometimes tangy taste. This milk was on its way to becoming a product like yogurt. Bacteria from the air landed on the milk. The bacteria digested the natural sugar in the milk, called *lactose*, and converted it into tangy lactic acid—a process called *fermentation.* When people make sour milk products, they can begin with milk, cream, or a mixture of the two. The end result is different depending on what you start with. If you add certain bacteria to milk, you will create a soft product such as yogurt or kefir. Add bacteria to cream and you can make sour cream or crème fraîche. If you add an acid, like vinegar, or certain enzymes to milk, you will create cheese.

A LUCKY ACCIDENT

Cheese was probably first made by accident long ago. Ancient people stored milk in bags made from the stomach of goats, sheep, or cows. An enzyme, called *rennet*, in the stomach lining of a young animal makes milk coagulate, or form curds and whey. Curds are semi-solid masses (such as cottage cheese), and whey is a thin, tangy liquid. People found that they could dry the curds further to preserve them for a long time. Today, we know these dried curds as cheese.

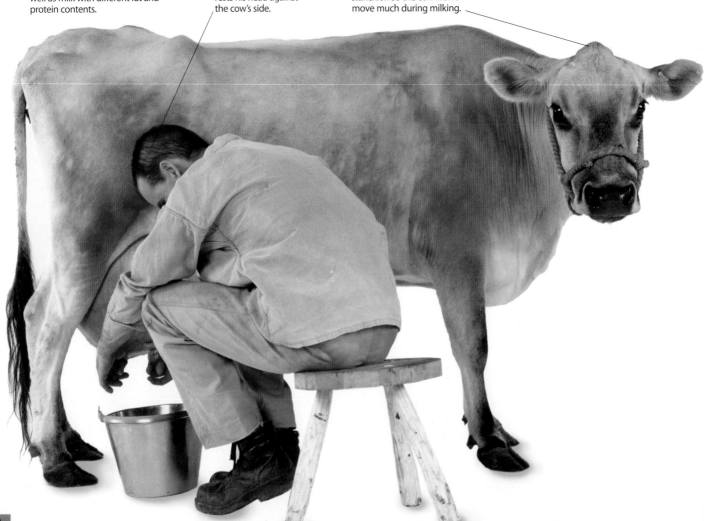

Different breeds of cows produce different quantities of milk, as well as milk with different fat and protein contents.

When milking, a farmer rests his head against the cow's side.

A cow's head is often put into a device called a *stanchion* so the cow won't move much during milking.

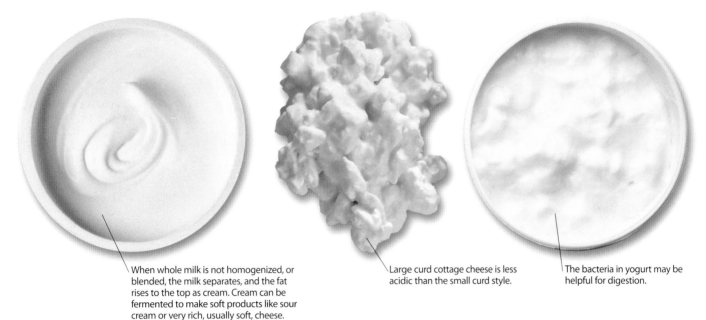

When whole milk is not homogenized, or blended, the milk separates, and the fat rises to the top as cream. Cream can be fermented to make soft products like sour cream or very rich, usually soft, cheese.

Large curd cottage cheese is less acidic than the small curd style.

The bacteria in yogurt may be helpful for digestion.

▲ FERMENTED MILK

Milk or cream that is fermented, or soured, by bacteria is sometimes called *cultured*. Bacteria produce the acid that sours the milk. Today, yogurt makers add different combinations of bacteria to milk in order to make it taste the way they want it to taste. The high acid content of yogurt keeps harmful microorganisms from growing in it.

MAKING CHEESE ►

To make cheese, milk or cream is fermented by the addition of bacteria or another additive. Adding acid or enzymes causes the milk to clump into curds. For some types of cheese, the curd is then cut into pieces, cooked, and salted, to make the whey come out of the curds. At this point, fresh cheese, such as cottage cheese, is ready to eat. Other cheeses, like cheddar, are pressed into blocks and aged for months or years to improve their flavor and texture before they are eaten.

A cheese maker holds warm, curdled milk that will become cheese.

◄ SLICING CHEESE

Cheese makers use many different methods to produce the huge variety of cheeses that are available. The flavor and texture of cheese is determined by many factors—starting with the particular grass or herbs the cow, sheep, or goat grazes on! The cheese maker shown here is cutting a mass of soft curds into smaller pieces. The amount of cooking, salting, and stirring he does with these pieces will determine how much whey is released from the curd. Once the curds are as firm as the cheese maker wants them to be, they can be pressed into blocks and stored until the cheese is ready to eat.

SPACE PROBES

Astronauts may get more attention, but probes are the true space travelers. Space probes have explored every planet in the solar system and many of their moons. Probes have peeked at the sun's poles, landed on asteroids, and captured dust from a comet's tail. Stunning images of distant planets are the most famous data returned by probes. But equally important are other kinds of data about a planet's magnetic field, the density of its moons, or the hint of water. The first space probes were launched in the early 1960s. Since then, probes have solved old mysteries and presented new ones. Even now, probes are speeding to the dwarf planet Pluto, to the asteroid belt, and to the outer reaches of the solar system. What new surprises will they send back?

did you know?
....
PIONEERS 10 AND 11 EACH CARRY A PLAQUE WITH A GREETING FROM EARTH TO ANY INTELLIGENT BEINGS THAT MAY FIND THEM.

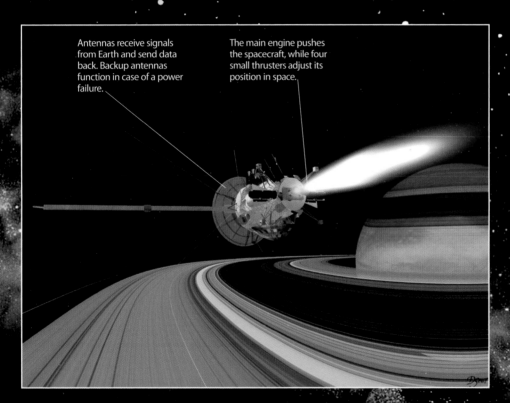

Antennas receive signals from Earth and send data back. Backup antennas function in case of a power failure.

The main engine pushes the spacecraft, while four small thrusters adjust its position in space.

CASSINI ▲
Starting in 2004, Cassini studied Saturn, its rings, and its moons. Its first mission, now complete, revealed amazing details about the Saturn system. The mushroom-cap-shaped Huygens probe—not visible in this image—rode piggyback beneath Cassini. Then it separated and plunged into the atmosphere of Saturn's largest moon, Titan. Cassini's extended mission is watching Saturn pass through its equinox, a time when Saturn's angle toward the sun is changing.

In the 1970s, Pioneer 10 and Pioneer 11 were the first probes to travel to Jupiter and Saturn. At first, scientists were not sure the probes would get through the asteroid belt, which is between Mars and Jupiter. The probes quickly scored many firsts, including the first close-up images, which revealed that Jupiter's mysterious Great Red Spot was a huge storm. Power sources on the Pioneer space probes eventually became too weak and the probes could not transmit signals. The two trailblazing Pioneers were last heard from in 1995 and 2003.

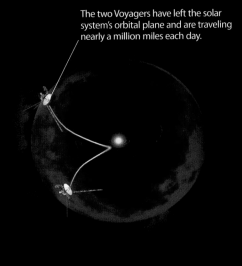

The two Voyagers have left the solar system's orbital plane and are traveling nearly a million miles each day.

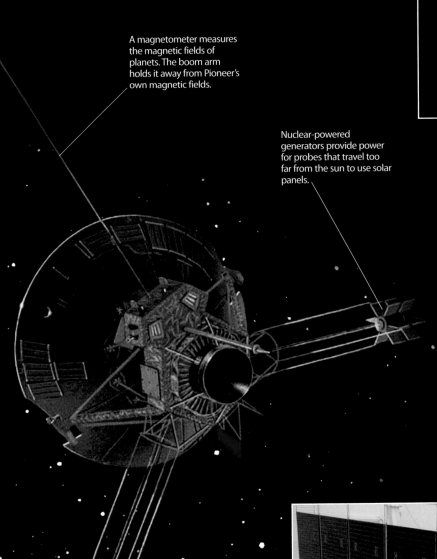

A magnetometer measures the magnetic fields of planets. The boom arm holds it away from Pioneer's own magnetic fields.

Nuclear-powered generators provide power for probes that travel too far from the sun to use solar panels.

VOYAGERS GO BEYOND ▲

Voyager 1 and Voyager 2 followed Pioneer's footsteps into the outer solar system. Since completing their mission to the gas giants—better known as Jupiter, Saturn, Uranus, and Neptune— they are on a new mission: discover the heliopause, the edge of the solar system where the matter from the sun is blown back by interstellar wind. So far, data from the Voyager space probes show that this is farther than predicted.

DAWN ▼

Solar panels provide power to Dawn's propulsion drive. Dawn was launched in 2007 to explore the asteroid belt's two largest residents: Vesta and Ceres. These two large asteroids are what scientists call *protoplanets*—clouds of gas, dust, and rocks that may form into planets. Data that Dawn gathers from these bodies should shed light on the solar system's early history.

Solar panel

SPACE TECHNOLOGY

Traveling to space and living there is no walk in the park. Because it is a vacuum, space has no temperatures. But objects in space do have temperatures that can be freezing cold or boiling hot. There is no air in space, so you can't breathe unless you carry oxygen with you. And there is no protection from cosmic ray radiation as there is here on Earth, thanks to our planet's electromagnetic field. When they go to space, people have to seal their body completely against these conditions. Scientists have developed ways to keep astronauts safe and healthy in space. Many of these discoveries are also useful here on Earth. Breathing systems for firefighters, instruments that allow surgery without large incisions, more comfortable shoes, and sunglasses that protect your eyes from ultraviolet radiation are only a few examples of space technology being applied to life on Earth.

did you know?
CDS, MICROCOMPUTERS, FLAT TV SCREENS, INVISIBLE BRACES, FIRE DETECTORS, ELECTRIC CARS—EVEN ENRICHED BABY FOOD—HAVE BEEN DEVELOPED THANKS TO SPACE TECHNOLOGY.

SLIDING THROUGH THE WATER ▼
Swimming is a great sport, but did you know that water slows down your body just as air produces resistance on the Space Shuttle? Water and air are fluids. They produce similar resistance to objects moving through them, called *drag*. The fancy swimsuits that Olympic athletes use were designed with the help of NASA's wind tunnels—research tools that allow scientists to study the effects of air on objects. The materials, the shape, and the type of seams used in the suits reduce the amount of energy a swimmer needs, letting him or her swim faster.

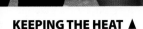

KEEPING THE HEAT ▲
During a space mission, spacecraft, astronauts, and equipment must be shielded from the dangerous rays of the sun. This is done with a flexible aluminized material that is lightweight, strong, and insulating. Back on Earth, this material also makes great insulating blankets for athletes, hikers, and emergency workers. The blankets, often called *space blankets*, can be folded to fit in a pocket, but they hold in heat as well as a heavy wool blanket does.

◄ THE COMFORT OF FOAM

In 1966, NASA began searching for a more protective cushion material for aircraft. The foam that was developed had a bonus beyond its improved energy absorption—it was more comfortable to sit on. The foam was used in astronauts' chairs, and then began to be used in wheelchairs and seating for people with disabilities. It took until 1991 for a manufacturer to find a process for making the foam at a price that consumers would pay. That material, which shapes to the body that sits or lies down on it, is called Tempur®. Now Tempur shows up in airplane seats, mattresses, pillows, shoes, and even inside football helmets!

Magnified Tempur foam cells

Tempur foam pillow

The sensor on the glove records the positions of the hand and fingers. It transmits them to the computer and then to the view screen.

The headset provides a three-dimensional view of the virtual environment. As the astronaut moves, the computer displays his interaction on the screen.

VIRTUAL REALITY ►

Airline pilots use flight simulators to practice flying an airplane. It's not the real airplane, but it sure feels like one! A simulator creates a kind of virtual reality—sights, movements, and sounds we experience that are not real but are provided by a computer. Like pilots, astronauts use virtual reality suits to practice space activities here on Earth. A computer coordinates their movements with the scene so they can see what it's like to work in space. Surgeons also use this technology to practice surgery, as if they were operating on real people.

SPACE TOURISM

The pilot folded the wings of SpaceShipOne® to slow his descent from space, and then opened them again to glide home to Earth. When he landed safely, in October 2004, his team won the $10 million Ansari X Prize®—and a new era in space travel began. It had taken eight years for a team to win the X Prize, promised to the first nongovernmental group to send a spacecraft with three people on board into suborbital flight (above 62 miles or 99.8 km, where space begins) and back again twice within two weeks. The winning team began planning and designing in 1996. In 2002, they started testing the parts of the aircraft: the craft's shape, engines, and how it performed under various conditions. Each test either confirmed expectations or prompted redesigns. Research and testing continued even between the two prize-winning flights. On the first flight, SpaceShipOne unexpectedly began to spin during its ascent. This problem was solved before the second flight took place. The goal of all this engineering effort? To make space available to anyone who buys a ticket.

JETTING INTO SPACE ▶

Virgin Atlantic Airways™ owner Richard Branson teamed up with aerodynamic engineer Burt Rutan, who designed SpaceShipOne. Their company is developing next-generation aircraft that will carry ticketed passengers into space. The new aircraft are scaled up from the technology that won the X Prize in 2004. From a space base in New Mexico, a carrier aircraft named WhiteKnightTwo will carry SpaceShipTwo® to an altitude of 9.5 miles (about 15 km). Then SpaceShipTwo will separate from its mothership and blast off into space, 68 miles (about 109.5 km) above Earth, using a rocket motor. One hundred people have already paid for tickets at $200,000 each, and even more have made deposits.

WhiteKnightTwo's single wing spans 140 feet (43 meters), connecting SpaceShipTwo (center) to two aircraft bodies.

did you know?
A FEW TOURISTS HAVE VENTURED INTO OUTER SPACE SINCE 2001, WHEN THE FIRST TOURIST—AN AMERICAN MILLIONAIRE—TRAVELED ON BOARD A RUSSIAN SOYUZ SUPPLY VEHICLE TO THE INTERNATIONAL SPACE STATION.

◄ STARFIGHTERS AND BEYOND

Starfighters®, Inc., explores commercial space travel with its fleet of second-hand NASA jets. The jet shown here just returned from a test flight that studied the impact of such flights on the area surrounding the launch site. Other companies are designing new equipment to bring passengers into space. XCOR® Aerospace is selling tickets to its Lynx suborbital launch vehicle, which is not yet finished, for half the cost of a trip on SpaceShipTwo.

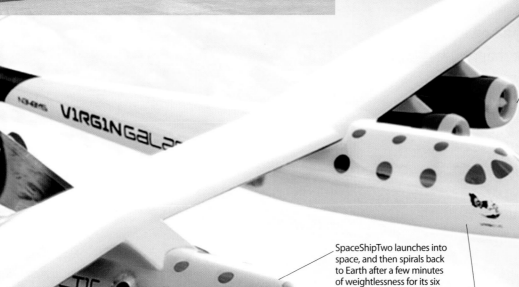

WhiteKnightTwo's turbofan engines are like those used in some private jets. Private jets use two engines; WhiteKnightTwo uses four.

SpaceShipTwo launches into space, and then spirals back to Earth after a few minutes of weightlessness for its six passengers.

WhiteKnightTwo's 2 cabins are identical to the cabin in SpaceShipTwo and will be used for passenger training flights.

SPACE HOTELS ►

Plans to build places where space tourists can stay are already in the works. This design for a hotel on the moon calls for it to be built from moon rock. The two slanting towers will provide space for moon sports, such as low-gravity flying. A hotel-chain owner has started a company to build inflatable space hotels. Two test modules are already in Earth orbit, with plans for larger facilities.

SPIDERS

It's hard to think of a creepy-crawly spider as an animal, isn't it? Well, it is. Spiders belong to the planet's most numerous and diverse group of animals: the invertebrates. Scientists have identified about 1.7 million invertebrate species, almost 40,000 of which are spiders. Like all invertebrates, spiders lack a backbone. Instead, they have an exoskeleton—a hard outer shell that protects them from predators, shelters their internal organs, and regulates water loss. Like many invertebrates, spiders are bilaterally symmetrical. That means a spider has a distinct front and back, and when you draw a line down its middle, the left and right sides mirror each other. Spiders are not insects; they are arachnids. Arachnids have two distinct body sections: the head section, called the *cephalothorax*, and the abdomen, or body section. Spiders also have four pairs of walking legs, two fangs called the *chelicerae*, and two pedipalps—leglike structures that function as sense organs.

The cephalothorax houses the stomach, brain, and central nervous system.

The carapace is a hard protective layer that covers the cephalothorax.

Pedipalp

The abdomen contains the heart, intestines, and reproductive organs.

Silk is produced by silk glands and spun with structures called *spinnerets*, which are located beneath the abdomen.

▼ SPINY-BACKED ORB WEAVER

Although spiders all share the same basic body plan, some are more ornate than others. The remarkable, tiny (2–10 mm) spiny-backed orb weaver is found throughout the southern United States and South and Central America. The female has 6 rosy-red spines protruding from her kite-shaped abdomen. Male spiny backs are smaller and less colorful than the females, and they don't have spines, just 4–5, small, abdominal humps.

The spines may serve as defensive structures that discourage predators from making a meal of the little spider.

did you know?..............
TARANTULAS CAN LIVE FOR MORE THAN 20 YEARS! THAT'S LONGER THAN MOST DOGS LIVE.

▼ JUMPING SPIDERS

With big eyes, fuzzy bodies, and flat faces, jumping spiders are pretty cute, as spiders go. Ranging in size from 2 to 22 mm, members of this family do not build webs to catch prey. Instead, they use their extraordinary jumping ability and keen binocular eyesight to pounce on prey with marvelous accuracy. Scientists believe that jumping spiders have the best eyesight of any spider. That's because they have rows of eyes on the front, top, and sides of their heads, so they can see close-up, wide-angle, and distance. Like most spiders, jumping spiders have four pairs of eyes, with each pair used for a different type of vision.

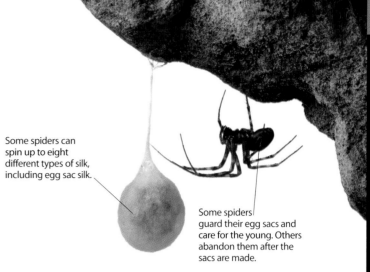

Some spiders can spin up to eight different types of silk, including egg sac silk.

Some spiders guard their egg sacs and care for the young. Others abandon them after the sacs are made.

▲ EGG SAC

Female spiders lay hundreds to thousands of eggs in silken sacs. These egg sacs keep the eggs warm and protect them from predators. Some spiders attach the sacs to the bottoms of leaves or stones to hide them. Other spiders carry the sacs in their jaws or attached to their spinnerets until the spiderlings hatch.

STEEL

Iron, aluminum, magnesium, chromium. These are just a few of the elements in the periodic table known as metals. Most metals are in the form of a metal crystal. These crystals consist of closely packed, positively charged metal atoms, called *ions*, with negatively charged electrons drifting among them. This structure makes metal a good conductor of electricity and heat, and makes it possible to bend and shape metals without breaking them. However, most of the metals we use regularly are not single elements, but combinations of elements, called *alloys*. Steel is one of the most widely used alloys. It is mostly iron, a strong and plentiful metal. However, when first extracted from iron ore, crude iron (also called *pig iron*) is brittle. Adding small amounts of carbon increases the metal's strength and hardness. These steel alloys are called *carbon steel*. Other elements added to steel provide additional desirable characteristics. For example, adding chromium to steel provides resistance to rust and scratches.

EIFFEL TOWER ▼

The Eiffel Tower, a famous landmark in Paris, France, is made of puddle iron, not steel. Puddle iron is a type of wrought iron that was used in construction before steel. This low-carbon iron can be made by melting and combining iron ore with carbon. The resulting iron is strong and malleable, which means it can be rolled or hammered into sheets or bars.

WELDING ▶

Steel parts can be joined with nuts and bolts or with thick metal pins called *rivets*. However, welding is an effective and commonly-used way to join certain types of steel. Welding typically uses heat to melt the materials to be joined. An additional material may be used to join the parts. When cool, these parts are connected with a very strong bond.

◄ COILED STEEL

Steel, like all metals, is ductile, which means it can be pulled into long, thin, strong strands of wire. To make steel cable, these thin strands are twisted together to form a thicker strand. The thicker strands are combined to make a cable. Steel cables can support tremendous weight. For example, each of the four 15.75-inch-diameter (40 cm) steel suspension cables on the Brooklyn Bridge can support up to 24,621,780 pounds (11,168,252 kg).

The steel typically used in construction, called low carbon steel, contains between 0.05 and 0.30 percent carbon.

did you
know?

THE WILLIS TOWER (FORMERLY THE SEARS TOWER) IN CHICAGO, ILLINOIS, WAS BUILT FROM 76,000 TONS OF STEEL.

As an alloy of iron, steel corrodes less than pure iron would under similar circumstances.

The high heat at this point melts the steel, forming a bond that can be as strong as the steel itself.

STEROIDS

You hear about them in the news, but what are steroids? Steroids are substances that take many different forms. Some occur naturally in your body, like the hormones estrogen and testosterone, which regulate puberty. Steroids can also be manufactured and used to treat medical conditions such as asthma. Some types—called *anabolic steroids*—are used to build muscle, but they are illegal and banned in most sports. *Anabolic* means they increase the body's ability to change amino acids into muscle protein. They are chemicals similar to the male hormone, testosterone, and they may make a person stronger, but at a price. Abusing steroids can lead to serious health problems because they cause an imbalance of hormones and affect brain cells, which may lead to physical changes. In males, the testes may shrink and breasts may develop. In females, the voice becomes deeper, facial hair may grow, and menstrual changes can occur. Both men and women can experience baldness and severe acne. Teens who use steroids may stop growing permanently.

▼ SHAKE UP SOME PROTEIN?

Muscles are made of protein, so some athletes drink protein shakes to build muscles. But is this necessary? Many experts think athletes can get enough protein by eating a balanced diet that contains about 15 percent protein. Because protein powders, drinks, and supplements are not regulated by the FDA, a product could contain unknown or harmful ingredients that may or may not increase an athlete's muscle size.

MASSIVE MUSCLES ▶

Why do some athletes think they need to use steroids? Steroids build strength and increase muscle mass, thus enhancing athletic performance. Athletes who use steroids have an advantage over their competitors. Body builders want the bulky appearance that anabolic steroids cause in their bodies.

BEN JOHNSON ▶

Ben Johnson was a top Canadian sprinter in 1988. Fans called him the World's Fastest Man when he smashed the 100-meter record at the Olympic Games in Seoul, South Korea. But within days of his win, he was stripped of his gold medal and his world record when his drug test came back positive for an illegal steroid.

did you know? ....

SINCE 1968, MORE THAN 40 ATHLETES HAVE BEEN STRIPPED OF THEIR OLYMPIC MEDALS FOR USING ILLEGAL PERFORMANCE-ENHANCING DRUGS.

Steroids can cause severe mood swings that can lead to violence, as well as high blood pressure, heart attack, stroke, kidney failure, and even cancer.

Although steroids help muscles get bigger and stronger, they may make the immune system weaker.

STORM CHASING

The driver slows, peering through rain so heavy it blurs the windshield in spite of the wipers. The headlights reflect off a sheet of water across the road ahead. Should he try crossing? Just then, a fresh torrent of rain falls. The floodwater turns brown with mud as the roadbed gives way to the destructive power of the storm. If the driver had tried to cross, he'd have been swept away with the road. Flash-flooding scenes like this are common during storms. Knowing where storms will form helps people avoid entering areas where the risk of flooding is high. But the exact location where massive, destructive storms will form is difficult to predict. Trained storm chasers enter risky areas during weather events to collect data about storm formation, location, and movement. Information is shared in real time through radio, phone, and Internet links, alerting the public to ever-changing dangers.

ON A CHASE ▶

Storm chasers have different motivations for putting themselves in harm's way. Some, like these meteorology students, seek to understand storms better. Many are photographers or documentary filmmakers. Some storm-chase groups gather data as a community service, to improve storm safety. And chasing storms for the thrill of it is a seasonal hobby in some areas. The gear storm chasers take along ranges from digital or video cameras, radios, and a laptop to more sophisticated equipment like weather balloons and Doppler radar. Storm chasers also use video cameras that get sucked into the tornado. These cameras, housed in special waterproof cases with a bulletproof window, capture the scene from inside the tornado.

Lights make vehicles visible in poor conditions. Most chase vehicles carry lights for both illumination and visibility.

TORNADO TRACKING ▶

VORTEX2, which stands for Verification of the Origins of Rotation in Tornadoes Experiment, is a research program involving more than 100 scientists and crew using more than 40 scientific vehicles to chase and surround tornados. VORTEX2 is documenting tornados from the time they form until the time they end. Analysis of the data collected will help determine what causes tornadoes, how fast the winds are moving, and how we can better predict future tornadoes.

Antennas connect chase vehicles with the outside world through cellphones, mobile Internet, and amateur (ham) radios.

**did you
know?**......................................
IN MAY 2003, 543 TORNADOES WERE RECORDED—
MORE THAN IN ANY OTHER MONTH SINCE RECORD
KEEPING BEGAN IN 1950.

SUBMARINES

They are heavy hunks of metal, yet they float as easily as they sink. Submarines are undersea boats that move through water with ease. They can dive deep, rise to the surface, and move forward with the help of simple machines. One of those simple machines is the screw propeller, which helps the submarine move forward. Whether a submarine floats or sinks is determined by its density. Two dense metal shells, called the *inner* and *outer hulls*, help a sub withstand the crushing pressures deep under water. If a submarine were solid metal, it would sink to the ocean bottom. But a submarine is filled with other materials, including air, water, and people. Air is lightweight—it has a low density. Materials that have a density less than that of water will float in water. Thus, the hollow, air-filled parts of a submarine can balance out the dense metal parts and help it float.

ATTACK SUBMARINE ▶

Attack submarines are military craft that silently cruise underwater throughout the world's oceans. Since the crew cannot see where they are going, they use sound waves, called *sonar*, along with computers and charts to navigate, or find their way. Most attack submarines are nuclear submarines, which means they run on nuclear energy. Nuclear fuel offers a seemingly endless supply of energy for the submarine. The nuclear fuel heats water to generate steam, which turns the turbines that rotate the propeller as well as produce electricity. This energy can also be used to process seawater and produce a supply of oxygen and fresh water for the crew. Food is the only limitation to how long the crew can stay underwater. Most submarines carry about a 3-month supply of food.

did you know?
THERE IS NOT ALWAYS ENOUGH SPACE IN THE STORAGE FACILITIES FOR ALL THE FOOD NEEDED FOR LONG VOYAGES. CANS ARE OFTEN STORED IN PASSAGEWAYS, WHERE PEOPLE WALK ON TOP OF FUTURE MEALS.

◀ RESCUE SUBMARINE

How do you save people from a wrecked submarine? You send another submarine! This small rescue submarine can be launched from its carrier ship near where a submarine is in danger. The rescue submarine attaches to the escape hatches of the wrecked submarine and takes the crew to the surface in small groups.

Blade number, shape, and angle determine the force of the propeller.

PROPELLER ▲

Propellers can be found on airplanes, ships, boats, and submarines. A propeller has two or more blades that force a fluid backward. A submarine's propeller pushes water backward, which causes the ship to move forward.

▼ RISING AND DIVING

A submarine's ability to dive or rise is controlled using seawater. Water drawn into special tanks, called *ballast tanks*, increases the submarine's density and the sub dives. When water is blown out by compressed air, the density decreases and the sub rises. A balance of air and water keeps the submarine at one depth.

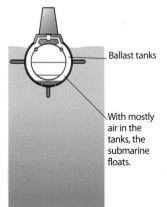

Ballast tanks

With mostly air in the tanks, the submarine floats.

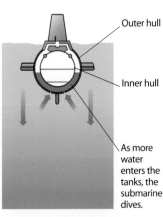

Outer hull

Inner hull

As more water enters the tanks, the submarine dives.

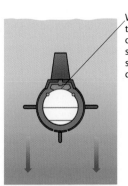

When the tanks are full of water, the submarine sinks very quickly.

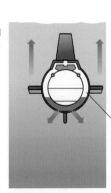

Pressurized air forces water out of the tanks, causing the submarine to rise.

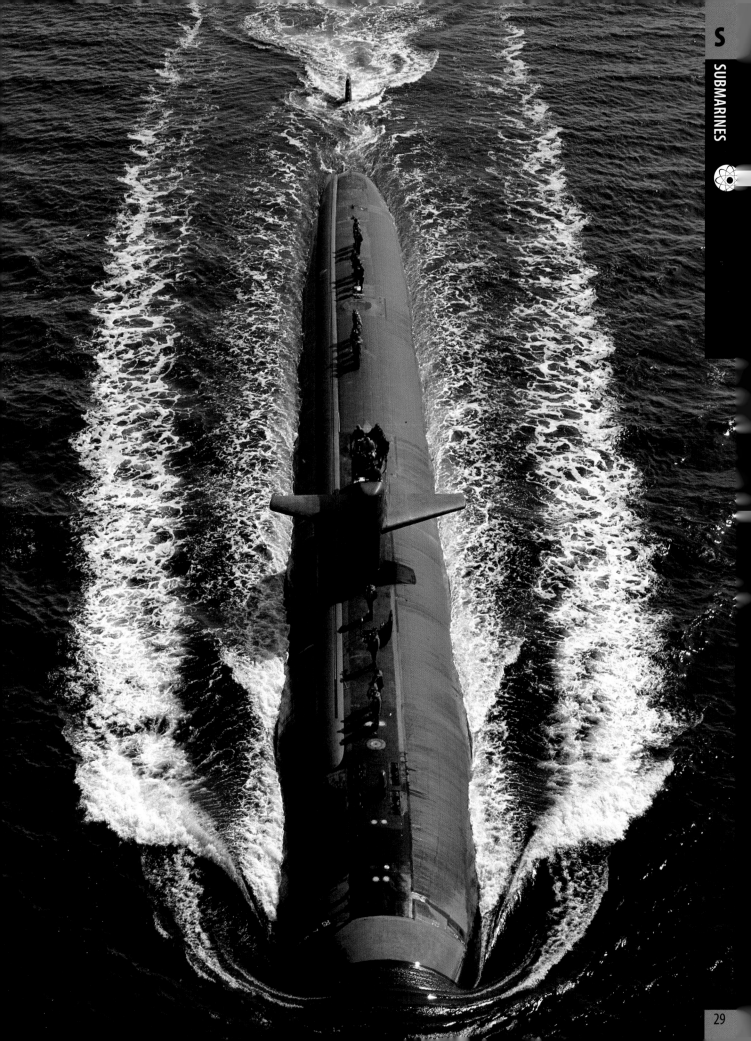

SUMMER SOLSTICE

Imagine you live in a place with long, hot summer days and long, cold winter nights. One summer, you travel north of the Arctic Circle. You notice that the sun never sets, not even at midnight! But even with all that sunlight, summer there is much cooler than early spring back home. In most areas, long days of sunlight bring hot, summer weather—but not at the poles. The higher the sun is above the horizon, the more energy Earth's surface receives. On the summer solstice—usually June 21 for the Northern Hemisphere and December 21 for the Southern Hemisphere—the sun appears at its highest point in the sky. But at the poles, this point is still lower than at any other place on Earth, so the surface receives less energy, no matter how many hours of sunlight there are.

1. The clock may say it's nighttime, but in the Arctic summer, the sun still shines high above the horizon.

SUMMER "SUNSET" IN THE ARCTIC ▼

North of the Arctic Circle, there is at least one day when the sun never sets—June 21, the Northern Hemisphere's summer solstice. The picture below was created from several photos taken on the summer solstice at the Turner River in Alaska, north of the Arctic Circle. The photographer captured the sun's position several times over a few hours to show its movement toward the horizon and then away from the horizon, but the sun never "sets" below the horizon.

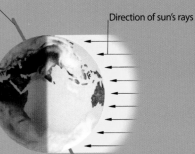

Because Earth is tilted on its axis, energy from the sun spreads out more when it reaches areas near the poles than it does at the equator. The greater energy at the equator makes temperatures hotter there.

Direction of sun's rays

SUMMER IN ANTARCTICA ▲

Earth's tilt always stays the same but the planet changes position as it moves around the sun. In this diagram, Earth's Southern Hemisphere is angled toward the sun. It's summer in the south and winter in the north. On this day, around December 21, areas south of the Antarctic Circle get 24 hours of daylight. Meanwhile, areas north of the Arctic Circle get 24 hours of darkness.

SUMMER IN SVALBARD ▲

Svalbard is the northernmost part of Norway, about 700 miles (about 1,126 km) south of the North Pole. In Svalbard, the summer sun never sets from mid-April to mid-August. This photo was taken on the day of the summer solstice. In this part of Earth, the rays of the sun strike at a low angle. That's why there is sunlight and also snow on the ground in summer!

3. It's early morning again and the sun is rising without ever having set.

2. The sun is near its lowest point in the sky. It's the middle of the night!

did you know? ....
NORTH OF THE ARCTIC CIRCLE AND SOUTH OF THE ANTARCTIC CIRCLE, THE SUMMER SOLSTICE IS CALLED THE MIDNIGHT SUN AND THE WINTER SOLSTICE IS CALLED THE LONGEST NIGHT.

SUPERCOOLING FROGS

Like all amphibians, frogs are ectotherms, meaning their body temperature depends upon their environment's temperature. Temperature is an important abiotic factor (nonliving part) of a frog's environment. How do some frogs that live in colder climates survive the freezing conditions of winter? The secret lies in their ability to freeze! Freezing typically damages cells—mostly due to ice formation—and can result in tissue death, such as frostbite, or death of the entire animal. However, some frogs have a secret anti-winter weapon. As soon as the frog's body detects ice, the frog's liver quickly produces large amounts of glucose or glycerol, which the circulatory system distributes to every part of its body. The glucose or glycerol is a cryoprotectant. It reduces ice formation in the cells and controls the freezing process. At the same time, water leaves the cells and moves into empty spaces in the frog's body, where it will freeze without damaging the cells. Eventually, the vital organs freeze and shut down, but the chemical interactions needed to keep the frog alive continue, even without oxygen!

SPRING PEEPER ▼
Amphibians have many ways of dealing with cold winters.
Some species of toads dig deep holes. Newts hibernate
underground in existing holes. Some aquatic species live in
the water below the ice. Spring peepers, frogs from eastern
North America that are about an inch (2.54 cm) long, can
winter in less protected areas: under logs or up in trees.

GREY TREEFROG ▶

Grey treefrogs inhabit eastern North America. They help control the insect population by eating mosquitos, flies, and gnats. When hibernating, they may burrow under fallen leaves or hide beneath loose bark. Both grey treefrog species—this eastern grey treefrog and Cope's grey treefrog—endure freezing in order to survive winters in the northern parts of their ranges.

The heart is the last organ to shut down during freezing and the first organ to start when thawing.

Ice growth typically starts in the frog's hind limbs and ends in the brain.

▲ WOOD FROG ON ICE

The temperature at which each of these frogs begins to freeze also plays an important role in helping them survive. A substance is supercooled if it remains liquid below the freezing point. The cryoprotectant in the frog's cells lowers the temperature at which the frogs will freeze. For each of these frogs, their bodies supercool only a few degrees before ice begins to form. For example, wood frogs supercool only to between 28°F and 26°F (–2°C and –3°C) before they start freezing. This reduces the possibility of ice growing too quickly, damaging the organism. Instead, the process of ice formation is carefully controlled.

SUPERFOODS

Our bodies require various nutrients—substances that supply us with the materials and energy necessary to live. We get most of these nutrients from the food we eat. So what is a "superfood"? Doctors and nutritionists don't always agree on which foods are "super." But in general, a food that is called a superfood has certain characteristics. It is a very good source of nutrients. It may help lower our risk of heart disease, cancer, and other illnesses. It is relatively low in calories. It can improve our health. It is also typically found in your local supermarket. Most superfoods are whole foods—meaning foods in their natural form. How foods are cooked or processed affects their nutritional value. After all, just because you eat a piece of carrot cake doesn't mean you get to skip your veggies!

FIT FAT ▲
A healthy diet contains some fat, but not all fats are good for you. Most of the fat in olive oil is unsaturated fat, which can help prevent heart disease.

IN THE PINK ▶
Protein, minerals, and fat are three types of nutrients our bodies need. Salmon contains protein, needed for growth and iron, needed by red blood cells. Salmon and a few other types of cold-water fish also contain certain omega-3 fatty acids—a type of fat our bodies need but can't produce. These fatty acids may lower our risk of heart disease, reduce inflammation, and support brain function. So don't forget the salmon!

did you know? MOST FRUITS AND VEGETABLES ARE MADE UP OF 80 TO 95 PERCENT WATER.

Eating tomatoes has been linked to a lower risk of developing certain types of cancers.

Avocados contain lutein, which helps keep your eyes healthy.

VARY THE VEGGIES
Vegetables are a great source of nutrients, including vitamins and minerals. Take broccoli, for example. Like other dark green vegetables, it contains calcium. It provides vitamin A, which is good for your bones and skin. And, like other members of the cabbage family, broccoli provides vitamin C. Some studies show broccoli may reduce your risk of cancer.

◄ MAKE ROOM FOR MUSHROOMS

Mushrooms contain B vitamins, fiber to help your digestive system work properly, and the minerals potassium and selenium. Potassium is necessary for kidney and muscle function, and selenium may reduce the risk of certain cancers. Most mushrooms also contain copper, which may be good for your heart's health.

FULL OF BEANS ▲

Beans are high in another necessary nutrient: carbohydrates, which provide your body with energy. Beans also contain protein, potassium, and magnesium, needed for muscle and nerve function. They're also a great source of fiber. Some beans, such as soybeans, have omega-3 fatty acids, too.

GO NUTS ►

Yes, nuts are high in fat, so they should be eaten in moderation. But their fats are good for your heart. And nuts are high in fiber, protein, and antioxidants, which repair cell damage and improve your ability to fight infections. Nuts and seeds, as well as nut butters, belong to this group.

Drinking tea may reduce the risk of certain types of cancers and heart disease.

Yogurt provides potassium, protein, and calcium. Calcium builds strong bones and teeth.

One guideline suggests you drink one 8-ounce glass of water between each meal; one with each meal; and before, during, and after exercise. Doing this can help you remember to drink about 2 quarts (1.9 L) each day.

BE A GOOD EGG ▲

Have an egg. They are full of protein. They are also a good source of vitamins and minerals, including choline, which may help the brain function better.

Among other vitamins and minerals, garlic contains vitamins B6 and C. And it makes food taste delicious!

WET YOUR WHISTLE ►

Water is our most important nutrient. It helps our bodies carry and use other nutrients, adjusts our temperature, and gets rid of wastes. Because we lose water every day, we must drink it regularly.

SURFING

Why would a surfer in California want to know what happened to a storm that was off the coast of New Zealand three days ago? Because waves from that storm might break on the California beach today. The surfer shown here off the south coast of Australia catches a wave that likely came in from Antarctica. Surfers are looking not just for choppy waters caused by local winds, but for swells, which are waves that travel deep in the ocean for long distances. Three factors determine the nature of the swells: wind speed where the wave originates; the length of time the wind continues to blow; and the expanse of the ocean over which the wind blows, called *fetch*. Ideally, the surfer in California would like to hear that a storm with winds of 60 miles per hour (about 96.6 km/h) was blowing for 36 hours across a 600-mile (about 966-km) fetch. Those winds would be strong enough to generate swells that could keep moving, merge with other swells, and travel thousands of miles for the surfer in California to catch a wave.

Oahu, Hawaii	SURF REPORT	Saturday, November 21
SWL HGT	Open ocean swell height measured from trough to crest in feet located 20 nautical miles offshore	7
DMNT DIR	Dominant direction typically +/- 10 degrees in 16 compass points	NW
DMNT PD	Dominant periods in seconds	18
H1/3	Significant wave height in the surf zone	14
H1/10	Average height of the highest one-tenth waves in the surf zone	18
HGT TEND	Height tendency of swell (valid values: up/down/same)	UP
PROB	Probability of occurrence (valid values: high/med/low)	HIGH
WIND SPD	Open water wind speed measured in knots located 20 nautical miles offshore	17–21
WIND DIR	Wind direction in 16 compass points	E
SPD TEND	Wind speed tendency (valid values: up/down/same)	DOWN

Surfers check the wind and wave conditions in the surf report before venturing out.

THE SWELL REPORT ▲

The chart above explains the abbreviations used in a surf report and the surf forecast for Oahu, Hawaii. Surfers need to know the height of the swells (SWL HGT) and how much time passes between swells—called the *dominant period* (DMNT PD). This surf report says that the surf is "7 feet at 18 seconds." This means that the average height of a swell in the open ocean is 7 feet (about 2.13 m) and swells are coming in every 18 seconds. Surfers are also interested in the significant wave height in the surf zone (H1/3). It is the predicted height of a surf wave, shown here to be 14 feet (about 4.27 m).

Wave height is measured on the face, or front, of the wave.

MAKING WAVES ▶

Where the wind touches the surface of the ocean, it transfers energy to the water. This energy moves in waves. If you could watch one drop of water in a wave, you would see it move in a small vertical circle. The particle does not continue to move forward with the wave. The energy of the wave moves from particle to particle of water.

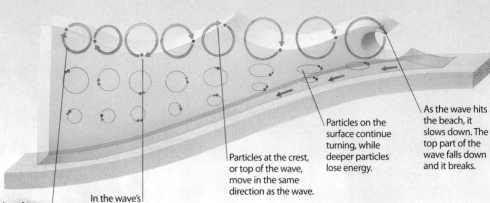

Particles on the surface continue turning, while deeper particles lose energy.

As the wave hits the beach, it slows down. The top part of the wave falls down and it breaks.

Particles at the crest, or top of the wave, move in the same direction as the wave.

Particles of water move in small, vertical circles.

In the wave's trough, or low point, particles move in the opposite direction from the wave.

Surfers balance by keeping their arms and legs flexed.

The nose of the surfboard has to stay above the surface of the water.

▲ CATCHING A WAVE

As swells move through the ocean, they sort themselves naturally by their speed. They form groups, or sets, of waves. As these waves move toward shore, their shape is influenced by the ocean floor they travel over. When the ocean floor rises steeply, the waves also rise steeply. Surfers look for waves that peel, which means they come toward shore at an angle and start to break at one end first. Coral reefs, sandbars, or other underwater features can cause waves to peel gradually from one end to the other rather than crash down all at once.

When the top of the wave becomes too heavy and full of water, it falls down, or breaks.

did you know? ONE OF THE BIGGEST WAVES EVER SURFED WAS AT CORTES BANK, OFF THE COAST OF CALIFORNIA. THE WAVE MEASURED 70 FEET (ABOUT 21 M) FROM THE TROUGH TO THE CREST.

SURVIVAL

Imagine that you are stranded on an uninhabited island. You have only the clothes you are wearing and a limited supply of food and water in your pack. It may be days before anyone finds you. What do you need to survive until then? All living things have the same basic needs, whether the organism is a plant, animal, bacteria, or human. For most, food, water, shelter, and air are just some basic needs. Organisms also need a living space, or habitat, that provides the food, water, and shelter. Maintaining homeostasis is also critical. Homeostasis is the state of balance inside an organism's body. It regulates conditions like body temperature and water balance. For you, it means things like sweating to cool your body when it starts to overheat, shivering to generate warmth when it gets cold, and feeling thirsty when your body is dehydrated.

SHELTER ▲
Shelter protects organisms and their young from predators and other danger. It also provides cover in bad weather or intense heat, and offers space to store food and other necessities. Shelter types range from caves, overhangs, thickets, and trees to constructed shelters like lean-tos, animal pens, and houses.

Although many people think a camel's hump carries water, the hump is actually a store of fat. This fat storage allows a camel to go up to two weeks without eating.

◄ WATER

Water is the most important nutrient. Without it, no organism can survive. Some animals get all the water they need from food. Most animals, including camels and humans, must also drink water. Human bodies are about 65 percent water. We need water to transport nutrients and oxygen to our cells, remove wastes, regulate temperature, and participate in the thousands of chemical reactions that occur in our bodies.

Polar bears usually eat seals, but they also catch fish. In summer, they eat berries and other plants.

The Inuit live near the Arctic Circle. Clothing keeps these children warm when temperatures drop below zero. Although most clothing is now store bought, the Inuit still make some of their warmest clothing from the fur of caribou and other animals.

FOOD ▲

Food is a source of energy that all organisms need to survive. Plants make their own food through the process of photosynthesis, but animals must eat other organisms to obtain the energy they need. An organism's cells convert nutrients from food into energy for growth, development, movement, maintaining a constant body temperature, and other life processes. Nutrients are also used to build and repair body and cell parts.

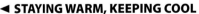

◄ STAYING WARM, KEEPING COOL

Endothermic animals, like cats, birds, and humans, are able to maintain a constant body temperature. Most stay warm with hair, fur, feathers, or blubber (body fat). Humans often have to pull on clothes, shoes, and other garments for extra warmth. To stay cool, endothermic animals sweat, pant, or shed fur. (We shed clothes!) Ectothermic animals, like snakes, take on the temperature of their environment. They are hot when it's hot outside and cold when it's cold.

SUSHI

It's beautiful and nutritious. The colors are vibrant and the arrangement is eye-catching. This popular dish—sushi—began in inland China as a practical way to preserve food. Foods placed between layers of rice lasted because of natural chemicals the rice made as it fermented. When this method spread to Japan, sushi grew in popularity. There, where the ocean is an important source of food, seaweed and fish (both pickled and raw) became important sushi ingredients. Eating sushi is one way for people to obtain energy from the mass of living organisms, called *biomass*, in the ocean. Within the ocean, the transfer of energy from one creature to another can be shown as a food web. At the bottom of the food web are producers, organisms that absorb sunlight and become food for other creatures. Producers are plants, such as seaweed. When eaten, these producers provide energy for consumers, organisms that cannot make their own food, like fish and other animals. Sushi provides humans with energy from both producers and consumers.

did you know? THE WORD *SUSHI* REFERS TO ANYTHING MADE WITH COLD VINEGARED RICE.

Hamachi (yellowtail)

Ebi (cooked shrimp)

EDIBLE SEAWEED ▼

Seaweed is a producer in the food web. It converts energy from the sun into a source of energy for consumers. It has been part of the Japanese diet for centuries because it is so high in nutrients. For example, wakame seaweed is usually used in soups and salads. Nori are the thin, dried sheets of seaweed that are used to make maki sushi, or sushi rolls.

KRILL ▼

Krill look like small shrimp, but they have a saltier, stronger taste. Krill play an important role in the ocean's food web. They feed on both producers and tiny consumers. They are eaten by many different creatures, including fish, seals, whales, and humans. Studies of krill's nutritional and medicinal value are in early stages, but some countries sell canned and frozen krill (in Japan, it is called *okiami*). Health food stores sell krill supplements.

Salad made with wakame seaweed

Maki sushi

ALL ON A PLATE ▼

This plate contains two kinds of sushi. The roll at the back of the plate, maki sushi, is fish or vegetables rolled up in rice and a sheet of nori seaweed. Along the front of the plate are several pieces of nigiri sushi, a slice of fish served on a mound of sushi rice.

Spicy horagai (conch)

Wasabi (Japanese horseradish)

Gari, or pickled ginger, is usually served with sushi to cleanse the palate, or refresh the taste buds, between different types of sushi.

Ika (squid)

Sake (salmon)

Maguro (tuna)

PRAWN ▼

This common prawn is a species of shrimp. They eat small plants and animals, and are eaten by fish and humans. The Japanese consider ama ebi (fresh raw prawn) a great delicacy. It is rare, however, to find prawns that are of high enough quality to eat raw. Most often, prawns are served cooked as a topping for nigiri sushi.

SKIPJACK TUNA ▼

Found around the world, skipjack tuna (katsuo) is one type of tuna served in sushi. They typically grow to about 3 feet (90 cm) in length. Skipjacks feed on smaller fish, crustaceans, and mollusks. They are often the prey of larger fish and seabirds. The population of skipjack tuna is larger than that of some other types of tuna. Populations of bluefin tuna, one of the most highly prized for sushi, have dropped dramatically due to overfishing.

SYMMETRY

What do a sea star and a rhinoceros have in common? Both animals have symmetry, which means that half of their body is a mirror image of the other half. With the exception of a few types of animals—like sponges—most animals have either radial symmetry or bilateral symmetry. Radial symmetry is found in marine animals like these sea anemones and the sea star. If seen from above, there are several imaginary lines that if drawn through the center of their bodies would divide the animals into two mirror-image halves. The rhinceros, on the other hand, has bilateral symmetry, meaning there is only one imaginary line that would divide the animal into two mirror-image halves. Most organisms have bilateral symmetry. Organisms with bilateral symmetry typically have a head at their front end. Within the head, sensory organs and a mass of nerve tissue handle information and organize the body's response to that information.

This sea anemone's radial symmetry provides it wit h the advantage of catching prey on all sides.

On top, some sea stars are covered with a netlike pattern of tiny, spinelike structures called *ossicles*.

Like most animals with radial symmetry, sea anemones don't move around much.

◄ SEA ANEMONE

Sea anemones might be mistaken for plants, since they typically live most of their lives attached to rocks or coral reefs. However, they are actually carnivorous animals! Sea anemones have a single mouth at the top of their colorful, tubular bodies. This mouth is surrounded by stinging tentacles that the anemone uses to catch and paralyze unsuspecting prey that get too close. Within the tentacles are tiny structures called *nematocysts*, which inject poison into prey.

▼ RADIAL SYMMETRY

Sea stars, like the ochre sea star below, are echinoderms, animals with a hard covering and radial symmetry. Most sea stars have five arms. While moving, any one of a sea star's arms takes the lead and the others follow. To reverse direction, sea stars don't need to turn around! That's lucky for this one, as giant green anemones have been known to eat sea stars—although algae, fish, and crabs are more common prey. When these anemones eat creatures with hard coverings, they spit out the hard parts.

The rhinoceros uses its two horns (one is located behind the front one) to defend itself from predators and to fight other rhinoceroses over mates and territory.

Giant green anemone's mouth

A BALANCED BODY ▲

Like this black rhinoceros, animals that have bilateral symmetry tend to be larger and have more complicated body systems than animals with radial symmetry. The bilateral symmetry of the rhinoceros allows it to move quickly and efficiently. With a brain and sense organs located in its head, it can also respond quickly to changes in its environment, such as the appearance of a predator.

This is not a smiling face, but the ray's two nostrils and a mouth with teeth. This young thornback ray uses its mouth to feed on small crustaceans, like shrimp.

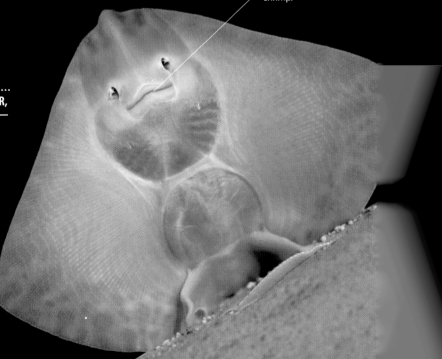

did you know? ....

AFTER THE EMBRYO STAGE, SOME ECHINODERMS, LIKE THE SEA STAR, BECOME FREE-SWIMMING LARVAE—WITH BILATERAL SYMMETRY—BEFORE BECOMING JUVENILES WITH RADIAL SYMMETRY.

BILATERAL SYMMETRY ►

This strange-looking animal is actually the underside (called the *ventral surface*) of a young thornback ray, a species of ray found in the coastal waters of California. Rays have very obvious bilateral symmetry. An imaginary line could be drawn down the center of the ray's body so that the resulting triangular halves are mirror images of each other. Bilateral symmetry is the most common form of animal symmetry.

TACO SCIENCE

When was the last time you looked at your dinner and thought about heat transfer? Heat transfer occurs when heat, or thermal energy, moves from a warm object to a cool object. Cooking food involves the transfer of thermal energy, which happens in three ways. Conduction occurs when a cool object, such as a raw egg, comes in direct contact with a warm object—let's say a hot pan on the stove. Convection takes place only in liquids and gases. When you heat water for spaghetti, for example, the warm water at the bottom of the pot, near the burner, rises and the cooler water sinks. The cycle repeats again and again. Radiation occurs when thermal energy is transferred by electromagnetic waves. Heat radiating from the oven walls helps bake a potato, for example. But did you know that heat transfer also occurs long before dinner ingredients arrive in your kitchen? Let's consider a taco.

The shredded cheese touches hot meat and melts by conduction.

Bacteria living in cattle stomachs digest plant cellulose to form glucose.

The bull eats the grass.

THE STOMACH IS CONNECTED TO THE . . . SUN? ▲
The sun radiates light waves to Earth. Green plants absorb the sun's light energy and convert it to chemical energy during photosynthesis. When this bull eats grass, the chemical energy in the grass transfers to his body. The energy transfers again, to your body, when you eat a beef taco. Digestion and cellular respiration release the energy, which your body can transform into mechanical energy to move your arm and pick up another taco.

Uncooked ground beef

Spices such as chili powder add flavor.

The ground beef changes color in a cooking process called *browning*.

Hot filling heats the surrounding air by convection. The warm air rises and cooler air sinks, cooling the taco.

EAT YOUR VEGETABLES ▶

Like all plants, the tomatoes, lettuce, and other vegetables used in tacos need light, warm temperatures, and rain to grow. The sun's infrared radiation warms the soil. Heat conducted by the soil helps germinate seeds. Convection takes place in the atmosphere, where warm air rises and cool air falls. Moisture in the rising air condenses into clouds, often leading to rainfall.

Mechanical harvesting, instead of hand picking, has increased the number of tomatoes produced.

Each corn kernel is actually a seed that contains an embryo and a food supply for use until the young plant can begin to photosynthesize.

did you know? ....
IN THE UNITED STATES, PEOPLE BUY MORE TORTILLAS THAN BAGELS, PITA, OR ANY OTHER ETHNIC BREADS.

Dried corn kernels are ground to make masa harina.

TASTY TORTILLAS ▲

Corn tortillas are made from masa harina, a special corn flour. The corn is air dried on the cob, and then ground into the flour. The tortillas are placed on a hot griddle and cooked by heat conduction. Sweet corn prepared for winter storage is dried by the sun's radiation or by convection in an oven.

TASMANIAN DEVIL

Temper, temper! A Tasmanian devil may look like a cuddly baby bear, but do not stand between it and its dinner. It will throw an impressive tantrum when someone tries to take its food. These carnivorous mammals are found naturally only on the island of Tasmania, a part of Australia just off its southern coast. Tasmanian devils are mostly scavengers—animals that eat dead things they find in their surroundings. Thus, they play an important role as the garbage collectors of their ecosystem, breaking down dead matter. Just larger than a house cat, a Tasmanian devil can be as large as 30 inches (76.2 cm) long and weigh as much as 26 pounds (about 12 kg). In spite of their small size, they travel great distances to find food. They may walk as far as 10 miles (16 km) in one night.

When a Tasmanian devil is about to fight, blood rushes to its ears, turning them bright red.

BORN INTO COMPETITION ▶

The life of a Tasmanian devil is rough from the start. Like kangaroos and opossums, Tasmanian devils are marsupials—mammals that carry their young in pouches. A mother devil births from 20 to 50 raisin-size young at once. However, she has the ability to feed only 4 of them. The young, called *joeys*, must race to beat the others to her pouch where they have a chance to survive.

Tasmanian devils are nocturnal and use their strong sense of smell to find food in the dark of night.

SCAVENGING AND HUNTING ▶

Although they sometimes hunt and kill fresh food, Tasmanian devils scavenge most of what they eat. They eat only meat. They eat every part of almost any kind of prey, and they don't care whether it is fresh or rotting. When several devils are feeding off the same dead animal, they will screech fiercely to protect their share of the feast.

During times of stress, a Tasmanian devil will give off a very strong smell.

This dead wombat was roadkill, which a tour guide left out as a meal for a lucky scavenger.

Sharp teeth and powerful jaws let Tasmanian devils tear apart their prey and eat even the furry hide and bones.

did you know?

TASMANIAN DEVIL POPULATIONS ARE DECREASING BECAUSE OF A CANCER THAT CAUSES TUMORS ON THE FACE, PREVENTING THEM FROM GETTING ENOUGH TO EAT.

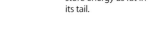

When a Tasmanian devil gets plenty to eat, its body will store energy as fat in its tail.

◀ CRANKY REPUTATION

The largest of the carnivorous marsupials, Tasmanian devils are known for their furious crankiness. They can be their fiercest and loudest when fighting with each other over food. Tasmanian devils let out ferocious snarls and bone-chilling screeches to show their fellow devils who is boss. Their famous open-mouthed snarl is actually a sign they are frightened or feel threatened.

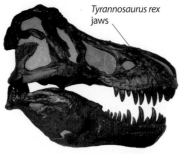

Tyrannosaurus rex
jaws

TEETH

Imagine how difficult it would be to bite and chew your food if all your teeth were pointy, all of them were flat, or you had no teeth at all. Although not all animals have teeth, most mammals do. Mammals can have four types of teeth, depending on the kind of food the animal eats. Incisors bite and cut food like raw vegetables and fruits. Canine teeth stab and tear meat and other foods. Premolars and molars grind and chew. Teeth have three layers. In mammals, the outer layer of these bonelike structures is made of enamel, the hardest tissue in the body. The main part of the tooth, beneath the enamel, is made of the mineral dentine. The pulp cavity is at the center.

Different shark species have different shapes and sizes of teeth, depending on the type of prey they eat.

FLESH-TEARING TEETH ▲

Scientists debate whether *T. rex* was more of a scavenger or a hunter. Either way, it needed its near-foot-long, cone-shaped teeth to tear apart flesh. Some of its teeth were serrated, like those of several shark species that use sawlike teeth to rip through skin and bones. Like sharks, *T. Rex* grew new teeth throughout its life.

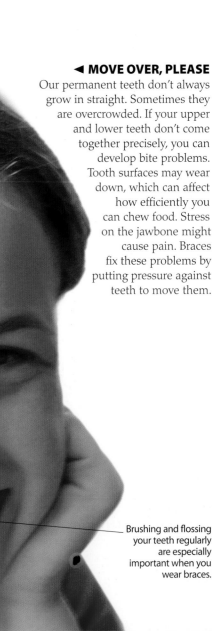

◄ MOVE OVER, PLEASE

Our permanent teeth don't always grow in straight. Sometimes they are overcrowded. If your upper and lower teeth don't come together precisely, you can develop bite problems. Tooth surfaces may wear down, which can affect how efficiently you can chew food. Stress on the jawbone might cause pain. Braces fix these problems by putting pressure against teeth to move them.

Brushing and flossing your teeth regularly are especially important when you wear braces.

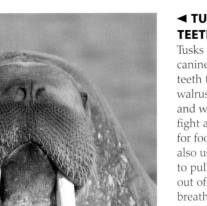

You can tell how old a walrus is by counting the growth rings in a tusk cross-section.

◄ TUSKS ARE TEETH, TOO

Tusks are elongated canine or incisor teeth that elephants, walruses, wild boars, and warthogs use to fight and to forage for food. Walruses also use their tusks to pull themselves out of water, punch breathing holes in ice, and rake through sand for clams. The strong flat molars inside their mouths crush snail and crab shells.

Herbivore teeth wear down at a specific rate. People who know about horses can tell a horse's age by examining its teeth.

HOLD THE MEAT ▲

Herbivores, such as horses, eat only grass and other plants. These animals don't always have canine teeth. They do have incisors, premolars, and molars. They use their incisors to bite off plants. Horses' molars are large and flat, with ridges and grooves for grinding up plant material.

A FULL SET OF TEETH ►

Mammals have two sets of teeth. Baby teeth grow soon after birth. The second, permanent set replaces the baby teeth. Once the permanent teeth appear, no more teeth grow. An adult human has 32 teeth. Because humans are omnivores and eat both plant and animal food substances, we have many different types of teeth. We can bite, cut, tear, and grind food.

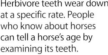

Incisors have straight, bladelike cutting edges for slicing through food. Incisors are the first teeth to emerge.

Canine

Premolar

Molar

did you know?

BALEEN WHALES, WHICH ARE AMONG THE LARGEST MAMMALS, HAVE NO TEETH. INSTEAD, LONG HAIRY PLATES CALLED *BALEEN* STRAIN SEAWATER TO TRAP PLANKTON, KRILL, AND FISH.

TERRACE FARMING

When it comes to agriculture, you may not think of mountains. But where there are no flatlands, and slopes are the only land available, farmers have learned how to make good use of them. Terrace farming is a method of growing crops on mountain slopes by building a series of low, flat ridges called *terraces* across the land. For thousands of years, mountain peoples in many parts of the world learned to build soil terraces on steep mountain slopes by containing the soil with big walls of rocks. For 300 years, until 1535 when the Spanish took over, the native Inca culture flourished in the Andes Mountains of Peru and Bolivia where little flatland is available. They built extensive terraces to grow great amounts of corn and potatoes. Properly built terraces slow erosion by stopping the soil from washing downhill when it rains. Terraces also allow water to collect and soak into the flat plots instead of flowing down the slopes.

MOUNTAIN TERRACES IN CHINA ▼

Many parts of China were once covered by forest. To feed China's population, many of China's forests have been cleared to make farms and rice fields. But when a forest is cut down, the tree roots that support the soil are removed, causing erosion on hillsides. Agricultural terraces can control some erosion, but walls made only of soil may collapse, especially if the terraces are made on steep slopes.

did you know?

IN SOME PARTS OF THE HIMALAYAS, FARMING TERRACES THAT WERE BUILT HUNDREDS OF YEARS AGO ARE STILL USED TODAY BY LOCAL FARMERS FOR GROWING THEIR CROPS.

Farmers' villages are next to the terraced terrain where rice is grown. These terraces can produce enough rice for people in the village to eat and to sell.

Entire mountains in China have been turned into agricultural terraces to grow rice. Terraces can hold pools of water. Rice grows in those flooded soils.

◄ FARMING IN MADEIRA

If you traveled the 36-mile (about 58-km) length of Portugal's Madeira Island, you would pass many hillside terraces. The origin of Madeira is volcanic and it has hardly any flatlands. In this mountainous terrain, farmers have turned as much of the land as they can into farmland by building agricultural terraces. Ancient irrigation channels bring water to the terrace farms.

In Madeira, farmers also build their homes on the terraces where they grow crops.

THE BENDS

Under pressure? Well, yes, you are—about 14.7 pounds per square inch (1 kg/cm^2). This amount of pressure, called an *atmosphere,* is exerted on your body by the air around you every day. But water is heavier than air. When you scuba dive, every foot you descend into the water puts more pressure on your body. This pressure squeezes your lungs and compresses the air inside. Air is made up of mostly nitrogen and a little oxygen. Oxygen is inhaled and used up by the body, but nitrogen gas is normally just exhaled out of your lungs. During a scuba dive, nitrogen is squeezed from your lungs and dissolved into your blood and body tissues. As long as you stay deep under the water, the nitrogen stays dissolved in your tissues. Returning to the surface has to be done slowly, with frequent breaks, so the nitrogen has time to reenter the lungs, where it can be harmlessly exhaled. However, if you rise too fast from a depth greater than 99 feet (30 m), the sudden drop in pressure allows the nitrogen gas to expand quickly in your tissues, forming bubbles. These bubbles cause pain in the joints, making you cramp up. That's why divers refer to this decompression sickness as "the bends."

DIVE BUDDIES ▶

The bends can cause pain, dizziness, shock, paralysis, and even death. To prevent the bends, divers must come to the surface slowly, making "safety stops" to let their bodies release the nitrogen gradually. All divers are advised to carry dive computers. Dive computers calculate when and for how long a diver needs to stop on the way up to decompress safely. This is especially important for professional divers, such as underwater welders, who go deeper and stay under water longer than recreational divers do.

DECOMPRESSION CHAMBER ▶

Treatment for the bends consists of spending time in a decompression chamber. They are made of steel, which is strong enough to withstand the changes of air pressure that are made. Decompression chambers are located at hospitals, naval centers, and aboard some ships. These devices try to mimic the pressure changes experienced in a safe, slow trip to the surface.

These tanks provide the air that is used to increase the pressure inside the chamber to match the pressure that the diver was at.

did you know?...
FOR EVERY 33 FEET (10 M) A DIVER GOES DOWN, THE PRESSURE OF THE WATER ON THE BODY INCREASES BY 1 ATMOSPHERE.

Divers use hand signals to communicate with their partners underwater.

Scuba divers breathe a mixture of gases, including compressed oxygen and nitrogen.

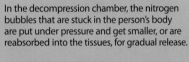

In the decompression chamber, the nitrogen bubbles that are stuck in the person's body are put under pressure and get smaller, or are reabsorbed into the tissues, for gradual release.

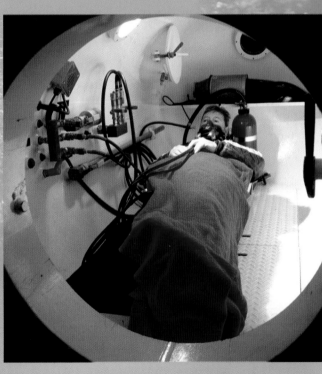

INSIDE THE CHAMBER ▲

To be treated for the bends, the person enters the chamber and lies down. He or she breathes pure oxygen, which helps the body eliminate the excess nitrogen. The air pressure in the chamber is high at first, similar to what the diver would have experienced underwater. Gradually, the pressure is reduced. Medical personnel watch the patient constantly. Treatment can take five or six hours.

THERMAL IMAGING

You know that some things glow when they're hot—like a red-hot burner on a stove or a white-hot light bulb. This glow comes from the thermal energy that is radiating from the burner or bulb. The higher the temperature of an object, the more thermal energy that object has. Objects around you are radiating thermal energy all the time, but generally not at these high temperatures. You can't see their thermal energy because the waves are in the infrared portion of the electromagnetic spectrum, a frequency slightly lower than the frequency of visible light. While looking through a thermal imaging camera, though, you can see those infrared rays. The camera's sensors can detect very small differences in temperature—fractions of one degree—to create a picture called a *thermogram*. Firefighters and rescue teams use thermograms to find people in a smoke-filled room or a dark forest. Engineers, doctors, electricians, and meteorologists are just a few other people who rely on thermograms.

ELECTRONIC CIRCUITS ▼

Electronic circuits pack a lot of working parts into a tiny space. If one of these parts gets too hot, the whole circuit may fail. How do you know when a circuit is hot or where the heat is coming from? Thermograms provide a heat map of the whole circuit while it is working. On this camera, the operator can see that yellow indicates a hot spot and blue shows where the circuit is cooler.

The blue in the background shows that the air temperature is lower than the temperature of human skin.

AIRPORT DISEASE DETECTER ▶

Thermal imagers are so sensitive to temperature that they can identify a person with a fever. Airports around the world have used these images to try to stop the spread of diseases such as influenza. The camera focuses on a person's forehead, which should show the highest temperature on the face. If the hot area spreads out across the forehead, nose, and cheeks, the person is more likely to have a fever.

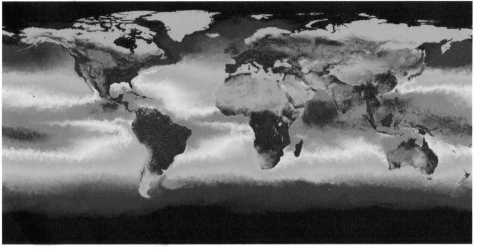

◄ TAKING THE OCEAN'S TEMPERATURE

The surface temperature of the oceans affects many of Earth's climates. Some satellites carry infrared thermal-imaging cameras that can continually measure the surface of the sea. In this image, changes in the map color from dark blue to light blue to yellow and then to red show the increases in water temperature. These measurements provide valuable data for studies of climate change. They are also used to predict changes, such as El Niño, that influence weather far from their location.

did you know?

DOCTORS HAVE DETECTED CERTAIN CANCERS AT AN EARLY STAGE USING THERMAL IMAGING. ABNORMAL CELLS FREQUENTLY EMIT MORE HEAT AS THEY GROW THAN NORMAL CELLS DO.

The screen shows each wavelength of infrared radiation as a particular color.

The scale on the right shows how color corresponds to temperature. Brighter yellow or green tones could indicate a person with a fever.

THUNDERSTORMS

Thunderstorms are nature's display of fireworks. They produce lightning and thunder, and are usually accompanied by rain or hail and wind. Beautiful and powerful, thunderstorms can also be deadly. Clouds form as moist air rises from Earth's warm surface. As the air cools down, the clouds fill with millions of particles of ice. Those particles collide with each other as the wind moves them up and down inside the clouds. This collision of particles is what builds up electrical charges. As negatively charged particles are attracted to areas of positive charge, they produce a large spark, which is lightning. Some thunderclouds build a negative electrical charge at the bottom of the cloud. This causes Earth's surface to become positively charged, through what's called *induction*. Negatively charged particles on Earth's surface are repelled by the like charges at the bottom of the cloud, so they move away. This leaves Earth's surface with a positive charge. When you see a lightning bolt strike the ground, you are actually seeing negative charges, or electrons, moving from the clouds to the ground. The positive ground charge tends to concentrate on elevated areas such as antennas, trees, or hills. Standing in such locations during a thunderstorm is very dangerous—you are an easy target!

A discharge of built-up energy produces lightning.

The longest recorded lightning bolt was 118 miles (about 190 km) long.

You see a powerful flash of light when the negative charge of lightning meets the positive charge of Earth's surface.

◄ THUNDER

The sound of thunder in the distance warns you that a storm may be heading your way. If you hear thunder, look for cover! When lightning flashes across the sky, you hear thunder a few seconds after you see the light. Light travels faster than sound, so the light of the bolt reaches your eyes before the sound reaches your ears. What produces the sound of thunder? Lightning heats the surrounding air, sometimes by as much as 50,000°F (about 33,000°C). That's almost 5 times the temperature of the sun's surface! This hot air expands very fast, causing a shock wave to radiate in all directions. The shock wave travels as a sound wave that makes the sound of thunder. Thunder makes a rumbling sound because you are hearing sound waves that radiate from different parts of the zigzag lightning bolt.

▲ THUNDERSTORMS ARE BENEFICIAL

Thunderstorms are beneficial to Earth in many ways. Lightning produces nitrogen oxides in the atmosphere that react with other chemicals and sunlight to produce ozone—the gas that protects Earth from ultraviolet radiation. Thunderstorms also help plants. Plants can't absorb nitrogen through their leaves but they can absorb it dissolved in water. Lightning helps nitrogen dissolve in water, which then gets into the soil. Finally, thunderstorms help maintain Earth's electrical balance. Electrons from Earth's surface are constantly flowing upward, and thunderstorms transfer electrons back to Earth.

Lightning is so hot it can melt sand and turn it into amazing glass tubes called *fulgurites*. These tubes form in one second and take the shape of the lightning as it hits the sand.

did you know? LIGHTNING FLASHES SOMEWHERE IN THE WORLD MORE THAN 3 MILLION TIMES PER DAY!

TOUR DE FRANCE

Exercise is good for your body and it's also fun. But competitive sports, like cycling, require more than just a healthy body. You need years of special training to develop your muscles and lungs for high-level performance. The Tour de France is the most famous bicycle competition in the world because it is long, tough, and very demanding, both physically and mentally. Competitors in this yearly bicycle race cross the French countryside and climb up and down its mountains in about 20 days. They go from sea level to as high as 8,000 feet (about 2,438 m), and then rush down at speeds of more than 50 mph (about 80 km/h)! Because the air gets thinner as they climb, these athletes must be in perfect cardiovascular and respiratory condition so their lungs can rapidly adapt to changes in atmospheric pressure and temperature.

Tour riders belong to different teams. Each team is distinguished by its jersey. Teams work together and support each other.

did you know?

AMERICAN CYCLIST LANCE ARMSTRONG IS THE ONLY RACER IN THE WORLD WHO HAS WON THE TOUR DE FRANCE SEVEN CONSECUTIVE TIMES (1999–2005).

The main group of riders is called the *peloton*, which means "flying ball" in French.

KEY
- **1** Start point
- **10** Rest/start point
- **•** End of stage
- —— Stage route
- ········· Time trial stage
- - - - - Transfer

1 Brest · **3** Saint-Malo · Paris
21 Etampes

2 Auray

4 **5** Cholet

Aigurand **6**

20 Cerilly
19 Roanne
Bourg-d'Oisans

Brioude **7**
18
Cuneo
Figeac **8**
Embrun **17** **16**
Toulouse **15**
Lannemezan **9**
Pau **10** **11** **14** Nîmes
13 Narbonne
Laveianet **12**

In 2008, riders toured France from the Atlantic coast to the Alps and south to the border between France and Spain.

◄ THE ROUTE

The route for the Tour de France, which changes from year to year, may enter France's neighboring countries of Switzerland, Italy, Spain, and Germany, but now it always ends in Paris. To get to the finish line, riders must endure a journey of more than 2,200 miles (almost 3,600 km). But distance is not the only challenge. The Tour winds through the mountains, where cold temperatures and less oxygen make cycling more difficult.

Traveling in another rider's slipstream, an area of reduced air pressure behind that rider produced by the rider's movement, helps conserve energy. Team members often trade places during the race to take advantage of other team members' slipstreams.

Professional tour bicycles are made of lightweight yet strong carbon fibers. The wheels can be changed for different road conditions.

To get the most speed from their efforts, riders crouch close to the handlebars in the most aerodynamic position possible. They also wear sleek helmets to reduce air friction.

▲ THE TOUR

The first Tour de France was run in 1903. Since then, it has been raced every year except during World Wars I and II. Each year, riders face sharp curves, steep slopes, heat, cold, high altitudes, and enthusiastic fans that crowd the route.

THE YELLOW JERSEY ►

Riders are allowed to wear a jersey of a particular color if they have the best score in a category on a given day. If they led in the mountains, they wear a red polka-dot shirt. The leader in points wears green, and the leader among those 25 and under wears white. The most desired of all the jerseys, however, is the yellow. It is worn by the cyclist with the best overall time. Different riders may take the lead on different days, and each of those riders will wear a yellow jersey. But it is the overall winner's yellow jersey that becomes a valuable trophy.

TRUTH IN ADVERTISING

What do advertising claims such as "low-fat" or "Earth friendly" actually mean? Until people agree on the definition of a term, these claims mean very little. In the United States, government agencies regulate the use of some terms. A product cannot be labeled "low-fat" unless it has been analyzed and shown to contain less than 3 grams (0.1 oz) of fat per serving. You cannot infer much from a label that says "Earth-friendly." "Made of 100 percent recycled materials" provides better information. And what if your favorite athlete advertises a certain product? Does that mean the product is good enough for him or her, or for you? Celebrities are paid for endorsing a product, and their endorsement can mean millions of dollars in extra sales for the company that makes the product. To be a smart consumer, it helps to think the way a scientist thinks: observing, testing, and researching to find the facts.

▼ TIME PRESSURE

Advertising doesn't typically focus on scientific testing of products. For expensive, highly engineered products such as cars, there are organizations that test, compare, and rate cars for several factors—safety, how frequently repairs are needed, fuel efficiency, and other facts that consumers should consider before they buy. But "sale" signs create a sense of urgency, making it less likely that customers will take the time to get the information they need.

did you know?.................................
ADS ARE EVERYWHERE! IN 2009, BRITISH COMPANIES SPENT MORE TO ADVERTISE ONLINE THAN ON TV.

Big red bows can distract consumers. When shopping for a car, people should look for the sticker on the car window that gives the facts, including price, fuel economy, and which equipment comes with the car. Then they can evaluate and make a choice!

BUY ONE GET ONE FREE!

This sale might be a great deal, but could you really eat all these oranges before they go bad?

◄ **SPECIAL OFFER**

How might you go about evaluating this 2-for-1 special? You would need to examine more than one orange in the bag. Are those in the middle of the bag squishy? You could compare the price of these oranges with the price of other bags of oranges. Did the store raise the price before making the special offer? And, can you fit this many oranges in your refrigerator?

Terms like *organic* can be used only if the product meets the law's requirements.

POWERFUL WORDS ►

How do you know whether the words on the front of a cereal box are true? By looking at the ingredient list on the side of the box, you can read what is in the cereal. The ingredient that is present in the highest amount in the product is listed first. The rest follow in order from highest to lowest. If sugar is the first ingredient listed on the box, the whole grain label might be true, but the proportion of it might be so low that the cereal is not a healthy choice.

This packaging label lists the nutrition information of the product. It tells how big a serving size is and the percentage of the average person's daily needs a serving contains. If you eat 1 cup of this product, you have met 47 percent of your daily iron needs.

Organic **Sunwheats**

Whole grain cereal
High in fiber to help reduce cholesterol naturally

Loved by professional athletes

NET WT. 12.4oz (352g)

Low fat

Nutrition Facts

Serving Size 1 cup (30.0 g)

Amount per serving	
Calories 110	Calories from fat 9
	% daily Value *
Total Fat 1.0g	**2%**
Saturated Fat 0.1g	**1%**
Trans Fat 0.0g	
Polyunsaturated Fat 0.4g	
Monounsaturated Fat 0.3g	
Cholesterol 0mg	**0%**
Sodium 210mg	**9%**
Total Carbohydrates 24.2g	**8%**
Dietary Fiber 3.0g	12%
Sugars 4.0g	
Protein 3.0g	
Vitamin A 10% *	Vitamin C 10%
Calcium 2% *	Iron 47%
* Based on a 2000 calorie diet	

NUTRITIONAL VALUES ▲

The law requires food manufacturers to list information about their product on the label. Consumers can find out how much protein, sugar, and fat a food contains. Some foods can have as much as 50 percent of your daily allowance of fat in just one serving!

TSUNAMI

The wind causes most ocean waves, but not the huge series of waves called a tsunami. Movements of the ocean floor—earthquakes, volcanic eruptions, or landslides—can cause these waves. However, most tsunamis are caused by earthquakes. Sudden movement of the massive plates of Earth's crust releases a huge amount of energy. The earthquake's energy is transferred to the water. The resulting surge can move at 500 miles per hour (about 805 km/h), travel hundreds of miles, and hit land as a 100-foot (about 30-m) wall of water.

A tsunami's destructive power can be seen in the debris, like this boat, that was tossed onto land.

1. Where Earth's plates meet on the seafloor, one plate is pushed up.

2. The water above the uplifted seafloor is suddenly pushed up.

3. The rising water causes waves in the deep ocean.

4. As the waves move into shallower water, their wavelength shortens and the wave height increases.

5. Waves become tall and destructive in shallow water.

◀ **THE POWER OF WATER**

On December 26, 2004, a tsunami in the Indian Ocean killed more than 200,000 people and destroyed thousands of buildings. It dropped this fishing boat on top of this house on the island of Sumatra in Indonesia. The earthquake that caused the tsunami registered 9.0 on the Richter scale and occurred about 150 miles (about 241 km) away from where the wave struck land. Huge waves also reached the coast of Africa, more than 3,000 miles (more than 4,800 km) away.

▲ **HOW A TSUNAMI FORMS**

Tsunamis travel quickly through deep water. The waves move in all directions from the earthquake's center. In deep water, they are seldom larger than normal waves and may not be noticed by ships at sea. Tsunami waves slow down as they run into the shallower water closer to land. The wave is compressed, forcing more water into each peak and trough. This causes the wave to grow dramatically taller.

did you
know?......................
A TSUNAMI CAN TRAVEL ACROSS THE PACIFIC OCEAN IN A SINGLE DAY.

TWEETERS AND WOOFERS

Tweet, tweet! Woof, woof! Music includes both high-pitched sounds, like the "tweet" of a flute, and low-pitched sounds, like the "woof" of a bass drum. The sounds travel as waves that cause nearby particles of air to vibrate. High-pitched sounds are made by high-frequency waves, and low-pitched sounds by low-frequency waves. When musicians record music, they capture the waves of many different frequencies as an electronic signal that represents the sound waves. To reproduce the original sounds—by playing a CD, for example—you need a device that can turn that electronic signal back into sound waves. That's what speakers do. But how can speakers reproduce the entire range of sounds from the flute to the drum? Most speakers do this by directing the high- and low-frequency waves to different parts of the speaker, called *drivers*. The high-frequency waves go to a driver called a *tweeter*, while the low-frequency waves go to another driver called a *woofer*.

HOW DRIVERS WORK ▼

The electronic signal that represents the recorded music is sent to one of the drivers, either the tweeter or the woofer. The driver consists of a set of magnets and a cone-shaped membrane. First the electronic signal moves the magnets. Then the magnets move the membrane, which is made of heavy paper or fabric. The membrane vibrates, sending out a wave that is a copy of the sound wave of the original music. The wave vibrates particles of air as it moves from the speaker to your ear.

The mixers in this recording studio allow musicians to separate and remix the individual sounds within the music.

Tweeter

The woofer makes the largest vibrations in the air, so it needs the largest vibrating membrane.

Each driver in a speaker covers a part of the total range of sound that people can hear. There are usually midrange drivers in addition to the tweeter and woofer.

▼ VOICE ANALYSIS

You know from experience that people's voices differ. You can recognize your best friend's voice in the middle of a crowd. The parts of your body that make the sound of your voice—vocal cords, mouth, nasal passages, teeth, and tongue—are unique. Scientists can use a sound spectrograph to analyze recorded words and identify the person who spoke them.

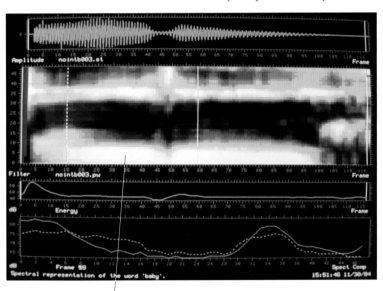

A computer processes the sound of a human voice and translates it into a series of graphs that represents the unique combination of sound frequencies in that voice.

did you know?

HUMANS HEAR ONLY PART OF THE SOUND SPECTRUM. ELEPHANTS COMMUNICATE USING VIBRATIONS WITH TONES TOO LOW FOR OUR EARS, AND BATS HUNT USING SOUNDS MUCH HIGHER THAN OUR RANGE OF HEARING.

◄ WOOFERS

For deep sounds, a speaker system has a woofer, named after the sound made by a large dog. Dogs have vocal cords that vibrate slowly, sending out a deep tone. The lowest sounds that most people hear occur when there are about 20 vibrations per second.

◄ TWEETERS

Like the chick, tweeters have small sound-making membranes that vibrate very rapidly. The highest frequency sounds that most people can hear occur when something, whether it is a chick's vocal membrane or a speaker cone, causes about 20,000 vibrations per second in the air.

TWINS

You might have some things in common with a sister or brother, but if you are a twin, one thing is most likely—you share the same birthday! Twins develop at the same time in their mother's womb. Identical twins, called *monozygotic twins*, come from a single fertilized egg—or zygote—that divides to form two embryos. These twins are hard to tell apart—unless you look at their fingerprints, which are similar, but not identical! Fraternal twins, called *dizygotic twins*, develop from two different fertilized eggs. They can grow up to be as alike or different as any two siblings. One twin might have dark hair and the other twin might have light hair. As fraternal twins get older, they are easier to tell apart.

▼ SHARING A WOMB

The mother's body provides the twin fetuses with nutrients and oxygen through the umbilical cords attached to the placenta—a mass of tissue linking the mother and the fetuses. Each fetus has a fluid-filled amniotic sac. In rare cases, identical twins share one sac. Each fraternal twin has its own placenta, but identical twins almost always share one.

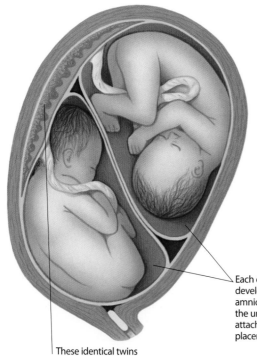

These identical twins share one placenta.

Each of these fetuses develops in its own amniotic sac with the umbilical cord attached to the placenta.

◄ TRIPLETS

Any birth that results in more than one baby is called a *multiple birth*. There has been an increase in multiple births in the last two decades in the United States. The chance of a multiple birth goes up with a woman's age, and the number of older women giving birth has increased. Also, the use of fertility treatments—a process that increases a couple's chances of having a baby—has increased. These treatments increase the possibility that women will release more than one egg at a time. Between 1980 and 2004, twin births increased by 70 percent. From 1980 to 1998, triplet births increased by 400 percent, but have declined slightly in recent years.

did you know?................................
OF EVERY 1,000 BIRTHS WORLDWIDE, ONLY 4 ARE MONOZYGOTIC, OR IDENTICAL, TWINS.

▲ ANIMAL MULTIPLES

For many kinds of animals, multiple births are very common. A group of animals born together to the same mother is called a litter. This litter of Siberian tiger cubs, an endangered species, was born in a zoo. Up to a point, multiple offspring can provide a survival advantage by increasing the chances that at least one offspring will survive. But the larger the litter, the smaller each individual in the litter, making the young more vulnerable to predators.

UNIVERSE

Miles and kilometers are fine for talking about places on our planet. They can even describe the distance from Earth to the moon or sun. But once you start talking about distances across the universe, these units are too small to be useful. Instead, scientists use the light-year, a measure of the distance that light can travel in a year. A light-year is equal to about 5,900,000,000,000 miles (9.5 trillion km). Numbers in the trillions are hard to work with, so scientists use scientific notation, sometimes called the *powers of 10*, to express these numbers. In scientific notation, one light-year equals 5.9×10^{12} miles (9.5×10^{12} km). The grids shown in the diagram below are divided into light-years or fractions of light-years. If you read the diagram from left to right, you will travel from Earth in the bottom left corner to the outer reaches of the universe, shown in the bottom right corner. Be sure to travel back, too!

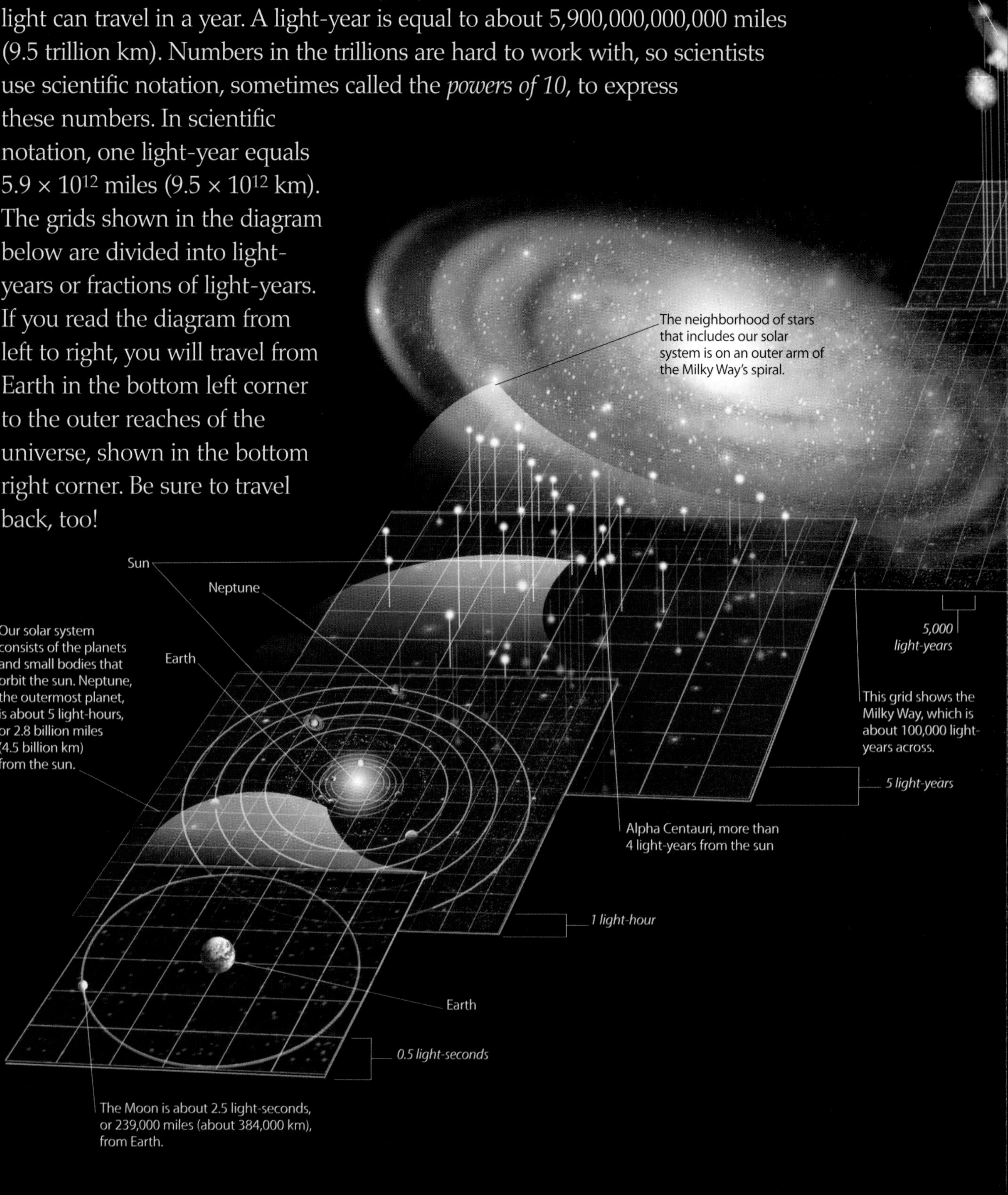

The Andromeda galaxy, the closest galaxy to the Milky Way, is 2.65 million light-years away.

The neighborhood of stars that includes our solar system is on an outer arm of the Milky Way's spiral.

Sun

Neptune

Earth

Our solar system consists of the planets and small bodies that orbit the sun. Neptune, the outermost planet, is about 5 light-hours, or 2.8 billion miles (4.5 billion km) from the sun.

5,000 light-years

This grid shows the Milky Way, which is about 100,000 light-years across.

5 light-years

Alpha Centauri, more than 4 light-years from the sun

1 light-hour

Earth

0.5 light-seconds

The Moon is about 2.5 light-seconds, or 239,000 miles (about 384,000 km), from Earth.

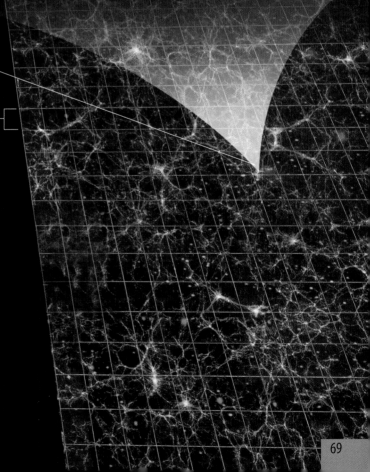

did you know? ECHOES OF THE UNIVERSE'S BIRTH DURING THE BIG BANG, CALLED *COSMIC BACKGROUND RADIATION*, ADD TO TV STATIC.

One group of galaxy clusters in the Virgo supercluster is the Local Group.

This grid shows one supercluster, the Virgo supercluster.

This grid shows just the clusters of galaxies known as the Local Group, including the Milky Way.

250,000 light-years

10 million light-years

Superclusters—clusters of clusters— including the Virgo supercluster, extend throughout the universe.

100 million light-years

THE OBSERVABLE UNIVERSE ▶

When astronomers look through a telescope, they aren't just seeing across great distances—they are looking back through time. The most distant objects in the observable universe—everything we can see—are about 13 billion light-years away. Working from that figure, scientists calculate that the universe is approximately 156 billion light-years wide. It's getting bigger, because observations show that galaxies are moving away from us and the universe is expanding. And suppose there were observers on a distant planet. The edge of their observable universe might be tens of billions of light-years away from them, with only a small overlap between our observable universe and theirs.

UPWELLING

Phytoplankton are tiny marine organisms at the base of the ocean food web. They are eaten by small fish, such as sardines and anchovies, which in turn provide a meal for larger fish, sharks, seabirds, seals, and whales. But what do phytoplankton eat? They don't really eat—they make their own food from carbon dioxide and the sun's light in a process called *photosynthesis*. Phytoplankton also need certain minerals. Sometimes, the phytoplankton are treated to an extra helping of carbon dioxide and minerals from the depths of the ocean floor. This process is called *upwelling*, the rising of cold, nutrient-rich water to replace a large layer of warmer water moved aside by the wind. Upwelling typically occurs along the western coasts of North and South America, Africa, and Europe, as well as along the equator.

16 March 2004
SeaWiFS Project
NASA / GSFC
ORBIMAGE

California coast

▲ UPWELLING OFF THE CALIFORNIA COAST
This satellite image shows an upwelling off the coast of California on March 16, 2004. The red and yellow areas are the richest in chlorophyll, which is a pigment in phytoplankton that helps the organism capture the sun's light. The nutrients carried by the upwelling cause the phytoplankton to bloom, or grow rapidly.

REAPING THE HARVEST ▶
An upwelling means dinnertime for marine animals, including predators large and small. Here, an increase in phytoplankton at the surface of the water has attracted hungry sardines, which have, in turn, drawn two copper sharks. The sharks have "herded" the sardines by circling them into what is called a *baitball*. Sharks and other sardine-eating animals swim through the baitball repeatedly, eating as many sardines as they can. At the same time, birds may dive in from above to participate in the free-for-all feast.

did you know?
THE 0.1% OF THE OCEAN'S SURFACE WHERE UPWELLINGS ARE MOST LIKELY TO OCCUR PROVIDES ABOUT HALF OF ALL OF COMMERCIALLY CAPTURED FISH.

Copper sharks feed mostly on fish like sardines. Upwellings make excellent hunting grounds for ocean dwellers, birds, and humans alike.

Upwellings off Peru's coast make the area one of the world's richest fishing grounds for sardine and anchovies.

HOW WIND MOVES WATER ▼

Coastal upwelling occurs when wind moves water away from the coast. Because of Earth's rotation and other forces, water moves at an angle of about 90 degrees from the direction of the wind. So, for example, a wind from the north moves the water either to the east or to the west—perpendicular to the wind. In the Northern Hemisphere, the water moves at a 90-degree angle to the right from the wind direction. In the Southern Hemisphere, water moves left from the wind direction. Below, wind from the north moves the water to its right—west in this case—away from the shore.

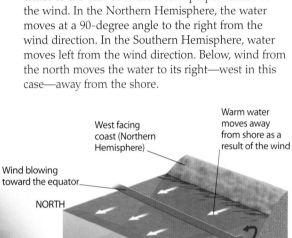

West facing coast (Northern Hemisphere)

Warm water moves away from shore as a result of the wind

Wind blowing toward the equator

NORTH

Cold water moves upward to replace the water moving offshore at the surface.

URANUS

Imagine the distance from the sun to Saturn: 941,070,000 miles (1,514,505,358 km) at its farthest point. Now double it. That's about where you'll find the seventh planet from the sun, Uranus. Like Jupiter, Saturn, and Neptune, Uranus is a giant ball of gas and liquid, primarily hydrogen and helium, with small amounts of ammonia, water, and methane ice crystals. Beneath the visible clouds is a layer of liquid—under exteme pressure—made up mostly of water, ammonia, and methane. At the center of the planet, scientists think there may be a rocky core about the size of Earth. Like all of the other planets, Uranus makes an oval-shaped orbit around the sun, which it completes in 30,685 Earth days (84 Earth years). What makes this planet different from all the other planets in our solar system? It spins almost on its side, like a slightly tilted Ferris wheel. Scientists hypothesize that, soon after it formed, an Earth-sized object struck Uranus, pushing it over.

Umbriel is a very old moon that has many large craters on its unusually dark surface. Astronomers do not know why Umbriel is so dark.

A layer of methane gas covers the clouds in the outer atmosphere of Uranus, giving the planet its blue-green color.

Ariel is Uranus's brightest moon, with perhaps the youngest surface. Its many valleys are marked with numerous small craters.

▼ **MANY MOONS**

Scientists have so far discovered 27 moons of Uranus—most of them named after characters from the plays of William Shakespeare. Uranus's five largest moons, the first two of which were discovered in 1787, are each less than 1,000 miles (1,600 km) in diameter. Ten of its smaller moons were first identified from pictures taken by the Voyager 2 spacecraft during its flyby of Uranus in 1985 and 1986. The smallest known moons circling Uranus are only 8–10 miles (12–16 km) across.

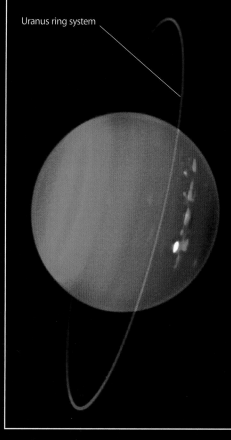

Uranus ring system

Titania is Uranus's largest moon and one of the first two moons discovered.

Like Umbriel, Oberon is covered with large craters. It contains equal parts of rock and ice, similar to Uranus's other large moons.

▲ **RINGS AROUND THE PLANET**

In 1977, scientists first observed the presence of the rings of Uranus when the planet passed in front of a star. With the help of Voyager 2 and the Hubble Space Telescope, scientists have identified 13 rings so far. One of the last 2 rings to be discovered is about 60,708 miles (97,700 km) from the planet's center.

The surface of Miranda is an unusual jumble of features, including both parallel and crisscrossing canyons and ridges.

Solar System

Mercury   Earth   Jupiter   Saturn   Uranus   Neptune

Venus   Mars

Sun

Uranus is one of the Jovian, or Jupiter-like, planets. It has the third-largest diameter of all the planets in the solar system.

VACCINES

Suppose a virus enters your body. This disease-causing pathogen has certain molecules, called *antigens*, all around its outside surface. White blood cells called *lymphocytes* recognize the virus by its antigens. Soon, lymphocytes called B cells begin producing Y-shaped particles, called *antibodies*. Antibodies are like puzzle pieces designed to lock onto specific antigens. Once the antibodies lock on, the viruses can't attack your body's cells. If the same type of virus enters your body again, your immune system "remembers" how to defeat it. This process gives your body what's called *active immunity* against that pathogen. Vaccines cause your body to develop active immunity to a disease without causing you to have the disease. A vaccine includes virus antigens that have been killed or weakened. They cannot cause the disease. The immune system, however, produces antibodies just as it would if the antigens were dangerous. As a result, a vaccinated person exposed to the disease is very unlikely to get sick.

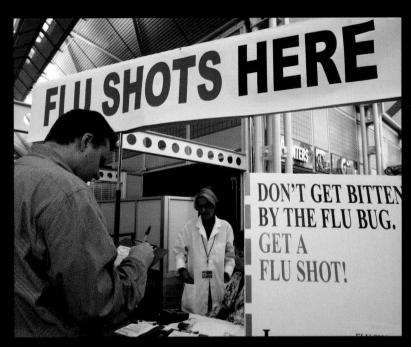

MASS IMMUNIZATION ▲

An epidemic—a widespread, sudden outbreak of a disease—often leads a country's government to set up a mass immunization program, in which everyone living in an area receives a vaccine. The vaccinations are usually given first to the people most likely to get sick and to those most likely to be exposed to the disease, such as health care workers. Vaccination programs have eliminated diseases, such as polio and smallpox, from many countries.

TESTING A VACCINE ▼

Before a vaccine can be used widely, it must be tested for safety and effectiveness. This woman is receiving a shot of a vaccine against the H1N1 virus, sometimes called "swine flu." About 8 to 10 days later, researchers tested her blood to see if antibodies against the H1N1 virus had developed. Antibodies had developed, showing the vaccine to be effective.

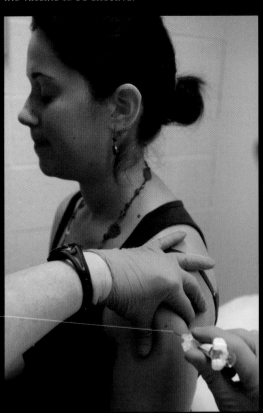

Influenza, or flu, shots need to be given yearly. Flu vaccines typically are changed from year to year to include the viruses that scientists predict will be circulating each year.

Both smallpox and cowpox viruses are members of the *Orthopoxvirus* genus. Vaccines are made using another member of the genus.

The smallpox virus's protein coat, shown in green, protects its genetic material and enables the virus to penetrate a person's body cells.

Viruses infect body cells and use the cell to reproduce their genetic material (red) and to produce more viruses.

The smallpox virus exists now only in a few research laboratories.

▲ SMALLPOX VIRUS

English physician Edward Jenner noticed that people who had suffered from the mild disease cowpox didn't contract the deadly disease smallpox. In 1796, Jenner rubbed infectious material from a woman's cowpox sores into scratches on a boy's arm. The boy became ill with cowpox. Later, Jenner exposed him to smallpox, and the boy did not get sick. He had developed immunity to this group of related viruses. Jenner's discovery has since led to the wiping out of smallpox, a killer of millions of people.

VENUS

Venus may seem similar to Earth in size and mass, but don't plan to spend your next vacation there. Its poisonous clouds of sulfuric acid, metal-melting heat, crushing atmospheric pressure (almost 90 times greater than Earth's), hurricane-like winds, and suffocating atmosphere of carbon dioxide make the second planet from the sun an unwelcoming place. The clouds of Venus trap the baking heat near the planet's surface, causing temperatures of more than 870°F (about 466°C). These same clouds also reflect lots of sunlight, making Venus one of the brightest objects that we see in the night sky. Venus has retrograde rotation, meaning it spins in the opposite direction from the direction in which it travels around the sun. This means that the sun rises in the west and sets in the east—the opposite of Earth. However, it spins very slowly, taking 244 Earth days for one complete spin. On the other hand, it takes Venus only about 225 Earth days to circle the sun. So a Venusian day is actually longer than a Venusian year!

VENUS EXPRESS ▶

Because Venus is so hot and its atmospheric pressure so great, studies of the planet are made from unmanned orbiting spacecraft. In 2005, the European Space Agency launched the Venus Express spacecraft to study Venus. Equipped with infrared and ultraviolet cameras to map the surface, the spacecraft has gathered important information about the composition of the atmosphere and the nature of the planet's magnetic field. Venus Express will send information to scientists on Earth through December 2012.

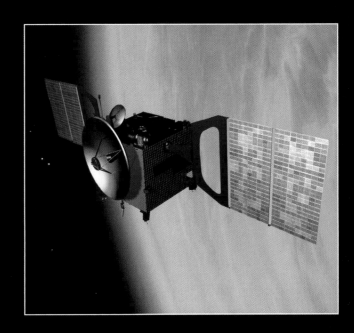

did you know?
....
ALTHOUGH IT IS ALMOST TWICE AS FAR FROM THE SUN AS MERCURY, VENUS IS THE HOTTEST PLANET IN THE SOLAR SYSTEM. ITS THICK ATMOSPHERE TRAPS HEAT NEAR THE SURFACE.

Solar System

Mercury   Earth   Jupiter   Saturn   Uranus   Neptune

Venus   Mars

Sun

During its orbit around the sun, Venus comes closer to Earth than any other planet, about 23.7 million miles (38.2 million km).

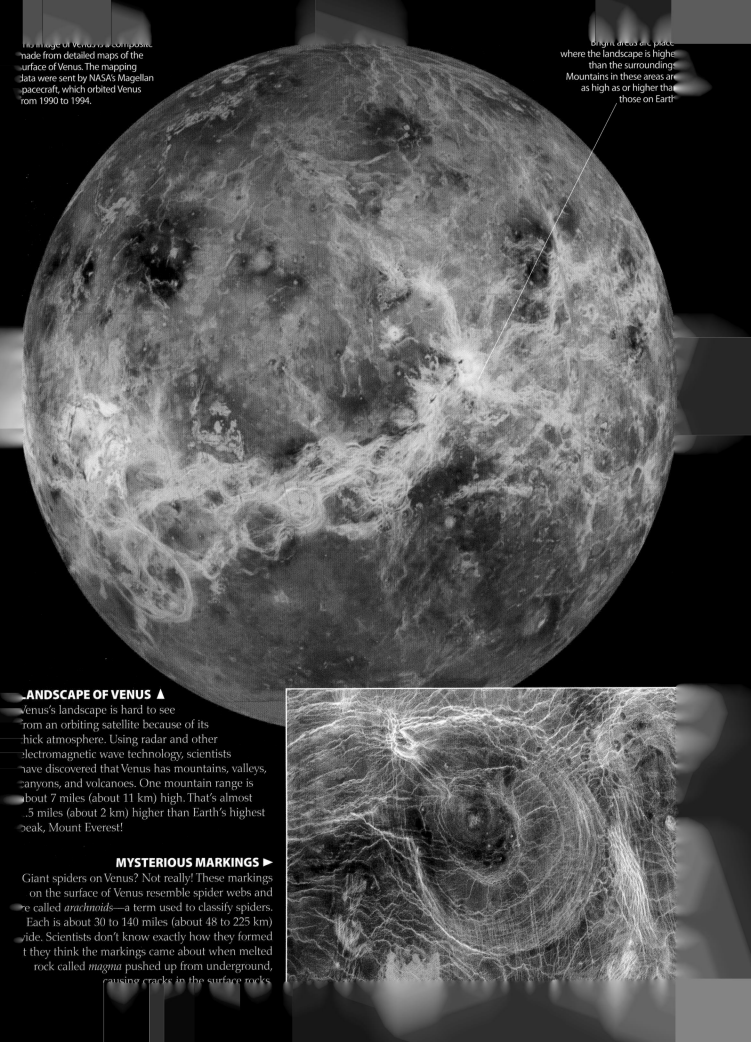

This image of Venus is a composite made from detailed maps of the surface of Venus. The mapping data were sent by NASA's Magellan spacecraft, which orbited Venus from 1990 to 1994.

Bright areas are places where the landscape is higher than the surroundings. Mountains in these areas are as high as or higher than those on Earth.

LANDSCAPE OF VENUS ▲

Venus's landscape is hard to see from an orbiting satellite because of its thick atmosphere. Using radar and other electromagnetic wave technology, scientists have discovered that Venus has mountains, valleys, canyons, and volcanoes. One mountain range is about 7 miles (about 11 km) high. That's almost 1.5 miles (about 2 km) higher than Earth's highest peak, Mount Everest!

MYSTERIOUS MARKINGS ▶

Giant spiders on Venus? Not really! These markings on the surface of Venus resemble spider webs and are called *arachnoids*—a term used to classify spiders. Each is about 30 to 140 miles (about 48 to 225 km) wide. Scientists don't know exactly how they formed but they think the markings came about when melted rock called *magma* pushed up from underground, causing cracks in the surface rocks.

VIRTUAL WORLD

Have you ever wished that you could drive your own car, have a pony, or go sky diving? You can—in a virtual world. A virtual world is a computer simulation, or model, of a make-believe environment. The space you see on the screen is made up of pictures, animated characters, and computer programs. A person participating in a virtual world is represented by an avatar, a computer animated character. Some virtual worlds are part of video games. But most virtual worlds use the Internet. Satellites allow people as far away as another continent or as close as someone in your hometown to explore the same world at the same time with you. Virtual worlds can give people opportunities to try new things, meet new people, and have fun. However, virtual worlds also present dangers. At times, a virtual world can become more important or real to someone than the real world itself. Some people worry that pretending to be violent in a virtual world could cause a person to be violent in the real world. Virtual worlds can also hide the identities of dangerous people, but as long as you remember never to give out your personal information, it is safe.

Some avatars do not represent a live user. Instead, a computer program controls what these characters say and do. This character may send you to find hidden items to earn rewards.

EXPLORING VIRTUAL WORLDS SAFELY ▶

The safety rules you follow in real life can be applied to making friends safely online. Never give someone your personal information, such as your real name, your address, your school, or your phone number. If the person online is not someone you know in real life, then all you know is that person's made-up avatar. Remember that it is very easy to "dress up" online as a character that is completely different from the person in real life. An avatar boy may actually belong to a girl. An avatar that looks 13 years old may belong to an adult.

did you know? VIRTUAL WORLDS ARE NOT JUST FOR KIDS. IN THE UNITED STATES, THE AVERAGE AGE OF A VIDEO GAME PLAYER IS 35.

Speech bubbles let users "talk" to other users by displaying the words above the avatar's head.

Users can often click on their avatars and let them interact with some parts of the virtual environment, such as hidden items.

Exploring virtual worlds together with friends from the real world can be one way to have fun safely online.

◀ AN AVATAR'S ENVIRONMENT

An avatar can move around in a virtual world and let the person behind the avatar—the user—interact with the imaginary environment and with other avatars. An avatar makes it possible to keep your real identity secret while still interacting with others. It gives you privacy and lets you pretend to be someone—or something—from real life. Avatars can be customized—made to have the same hair and eye color and look like the people they represent or made to look completely different. With an avatar, you can also safely try activities that are expensive or impossible in the real world. For example, in a virtual world, you could get an apartment and buy furniture for it. You could even get a pet chameleon or a puppy. Just don't forget to feed them. Virtual pets can get hungry, just like real ones!

Every player can choose a unique username, which identifies his or her avatar.

VITAMINS AND MINERALS

There are at least two good reasons to eat fruits, vegetables, whole grains, and other nutritious foods: vitamins and minerals. Your body needs both for proper growth, development, and function. Vitamins are natural substances made by plants and animals. They are also added to some foods, such as milk and cereal. Some—vitamins A, D, E, and K—are fat-soluble. Your body stores them in fat tissue. Too much of a fat-soluble vitamin can make you sick. Water-soluble vitamins, such as B and C, must dissolve in water before your body can use them. Your body doesn't store them. If you eat too much of a water-soluble vitamin, the excess is excreted in urine. Unlike vitamins, minerals are inorganic elements found in soil and water. Minerals are absorbed by plants and eaten by animals. Each vitamin and mineral has a special role in the body.

did you know?..........
HARD WATER CONTAINS CALCIUM AND MAGNESIUM THAT CAN CLOG PIPES. HOWEVER, WHEN YOU DRINK HARD WATER, YOUR BODY ABSORBS AND USES THESE MINERALS, AS IT WOULD FROM FOOD.

Romaine lettuce

VITAMIN E ▶
Vitamin E is an antioxidant. Antioxidants protect tissues from the damaging effects of unstable molecules called *free radicals*, which may play a role in aging and cancer. Vitamin E also keeps red blood cells healthy. Teens need about 15 milligrams of vitamin E each day. Eating avocados, whole grains, vegetable oils, and nuts provides this amount.

Nuts

Avocados contain a variety of minerals and vitamins, including vitamin E.

VITAMIN K ▲
Vitamin K was named for the German word *koagulation*. Coagulation means blood clotting, which can't occur without vitamin K. Vitamin K is also needed for healthy bones. It is easy to get enough vitamin K because it is found in many foods, including dark green leafy vegetables, olive oil, and soybeans. Bacteria in your intestine can also make it.

VITAMIN B9
Also known as folic acid, vitamin B9 is important in DNA synthesis and the formation of new cells. This vitamin is especially important in early pregnancy when an embryo is forming body systems and growing rapidly. Folic acid helps break down proteins and form new ones. It also helps form red blood cells. Broccoli and other green vegetables, citrus fruits, and beans contain folic acid.

Broccoli

Red blood cell

VITAMIN B12 ▲
Vitamin B12 is part of a group of vitamins with similar properties, sources, and functions. Your body needs vitamin B12 to make DNA during cell division. Vitamin B12 also helps maintain healthy nerve cells and supports the formation of red blood cells. Although this B vitamin is water soluble, your body can store large quantities of it. B12 occurs naturally in meat, fish, eggs, and dairy products.

Fish

All the foods shown here contain iron, which helps your body produce oxygen-carrying proteins in your blood and muscles.

Spinach

Meat

◀ IRON
Hemoglobin is the protein in red blood cells that transports oxygen from your lungs to your cells. Oxygen is used in cellular respiration to release energy. Hemoglobin contains the mineral iron. Without iron, your cells can't get enough energy. Adolescent girls need 15 and boys need 11 milligrams of iron per day. One hamburger provides 4 milligrams.

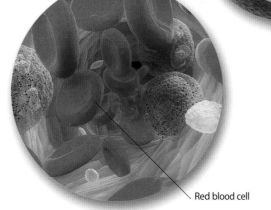

POTASSIUM ▶

So many foods contain the mineral potassium that it is easy for you to meet your daily needs. The flow of potassium ions in and out of nerve and muscle cells helps support a strong heartbeat, transmission of nerve impulses, and muscle contraction. Potassium also helps balance acids and bases in the body.

Bananas are rich in potassium, which helps your muscles and nerves.

Oily fish also has flourine, a mineral that is very good for teeth and eyes.

▲ VITAMIN D

Oily fish, such as salmon, sardines, and mackerel, are among the few food sources of vitamin D. Vitamin D is usually added to milk. Without vitamin D, the body cannot use calcium to build bones and teeth. Vitamin D also helps the immune system. The body makes some vitamin D when skin is exposed to sunlight.

Whole grains are good for keeping your muscles and bones strong because they contain high levels of magnesium.

▲ MINERALS FOR HEALTHY BONES

Almost all the calcium and more than half the magnesium in your body is found in your bones. In addition to keeping bones strong, these minerals are involved in hundreds of processes in the body, such as muscle and nerve function. Magnesium is in whole grains, but is lost when parts of the grain are removed to make white flour or white rice. Calcium is in dairy products, beans, and leafy greens.

Carrots help to keep your eyes healthy as they are rich in vitamin A.

VITAMINS A AND C

Vitamin A plays a role in vision and helps your body fight infection. Yellow and orange fruits and vegetables contain vitamin A. One sweet potato provides all your daily needs. Vitamin C is needed for growth and tissue repair. You need about 70 milligrams of vitamin C every day. One orange provides this amount.

Oranges are high in vitamin C, which keeps your teeth, gums, bones, and blood vessels healthy.

▼ VITAMINS B1, B2, AND B3

Vitamins B1 (also known as thiamine), B2 (riboflavin), and B3 (niacin) help break down carbohydrates, so they maintain your body's energy supply and help you grow. One pork chop has more B1 than you need in a day. One cup of yogurt supplies about half the B2 you need. One-half cup of peanuts contains about two thirds of the B3 you need.

Eggs contain large amounts of riboflavin (vitamin B2), which is also found in green leafy vegetables and dairy products.

Pork, grains, and beans are among the foods that are high in thiamine (vitamin B1).

Dairy products, lean meat, fish, and nuts are high in niacin (vitamin B3).

◀ SODIUM

Sodium is important for nerve function, but too much causes some people to develop high blood pressure. The nutrition labels on food packages list the amount of sodium in foods.

Salt

VULTURES

Despite the fact that they are well-recognized, vultures have really been misunderstood. Their associations with dead and dying animals have led some people to assume they are vicious, dirty pests. In reality, vultures help maintain the health and beauty of ecosystems by eating animal flesh that would otherwise rot and spread harmful diseases. Vultures also have some interesting habits. New World vultures—consisting of the seven species that live in North and South America—urinate on their legs and feet. The evaporation of the urine cools the bird and the uric acid in the urine kills bacteria. Some vultures defend themselves and their nests by vomiting at predators. Despite these behaviors, vultures are very clean animals. After eating, vultures preen—they bathe and arrange their feathers—and sit in the sun. The ultraviolet light kills harmful bacteria the birds may have picked up on their head or feathers while eating.

BLACK VULTURE ▶

Black vultures are one of the seven species of New World vultures. They live throughout most of South America, Central America, Mexico, and the southern and eastern United States. Because they rely upon their eyesight for finding food, black vultures can be found in open or lightly wooded areas, near the water, and in urban areas. In fact, large groups are often found scavenging near garbage dumps and slaughterhouses. Other New World vultures include the turkey vulture, the California condor, and the Andean condor.

WHITE-BACKED VULTURE ▼

The 15 vulture species that live in Europe, Asia, Africa, and the Middle East are known as Old World vultures. One of these is the white-backed vulture, named for its white lower back. It lives in various parts of Africa. Weighing an average of 12.1 pounds (5.5 kg), these birds can have a wingspan of almost 7.2 feet (218 cm). That is wider than most people are tall!

A long bill, as well as a long neck and small head, allows the white-backed vulture to reach deep into carcasses.

Bacteria-carrying meat and blood is less likely to stick to the bare heads that most vultures have than to long feathers.

CLEANING UP ▶

White-backed vultures feed on the bodies of large grazing animals, such as elephants, rhinos, and zebras. There may be hundreds of them scavenging the same carcass, stripping a large animal clean of meat in a matter of hours. Like all vultures, white-backed vultures have excellent eyesight, which they use to scan for food—or the sudden descent of other food-seeking vultures—while circling high above the savannah or wooded countryside.

While flying, black vultures typically beat their wings quickly several times in between short glides.

Some vultures, such as this Andean black vulture, soar on columns of warm, rising air currents called *thermals*, which keep them aloft for long periods of time.

did you know? WEIGHING UP TO 33 POUNDS (ALMOST 15 KG), THE ANDEAN CONDOR IS ONE OF THE WORLD'S LARGEST FLYING BIRDS.

White-backed vultures will often hiss and squawk at each other as they try to feed on the same carcass.

Vultures rarely eat live animals. The larger New World vultures may occasionally pick up live young animals, such as a lamb.

83

WATER

Each of us is made up of roughly 60–70 percent water. In fact, all life on
Earth owes its existence to water, a molecule that consists of two atoms of
hydrogen bound to one side of an atom of oxygen. Water is a polar molecule:
the oxygen end of the molecule has a slightly negative charge and the
hydrogen end has a slightly positive charge. This causes water molecules to
be attracted to each other. It also causes the particles of many substances
to separate from each other in water, a process that is called *dissolving*.
Because of water's ability to dissolve so many substances, water is essential
for our body's health. Most nutrients in the body are dissolved in water and
transported to cells. Wastes are dissolved in water and transported away from
cells. Water helps in regulating body temperature. Red blood cells carrying
oxygen are suspended in blood, the liquid portion of which is a solution of
more than 90 percent water. In addition, water plays an important role in
several chemical processes in the body. Water is needed to break down large
molecules, such as proteins, into smaller molecules, like amino acids, that
the body can use. Water is produced as a by-product when small molecules
combine to form large molecules, such as starches and proteins. Water is also
produced during cellular respiration, the process by which a cell breaks down
glucose to get energy.

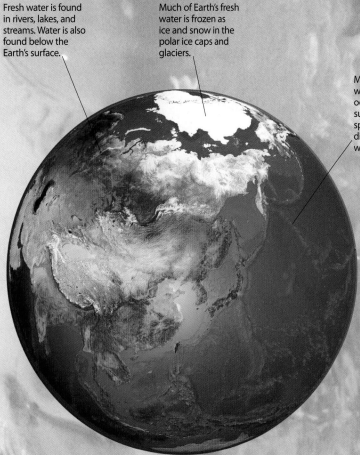

Fresh water is found
in rivers, lakes, and
streams. Water is also
found below the
Earth's surface.

Much of Earth's fresh
water is frozen as
ice and snow in the
polar ice caps and
glaciers.

Most of Earth's
water is found in the
ocean. Many salts,
such as the salt you
sprinkle on food, are
dissolved in ocean
water.

◄ HOW MUCH WATER?

About 5 hours into their trip to the moon, the
astronauts on board Apollo 17 took several pictures
of Earth. Earth appears blue because almost three
fourths of its surface is water. Almost 97 percent
of Earth's water is in the oceans. Most of the fresh
water is frozen in the polar ice caps, glaciers, and
snow. That leaves about 1 percent of Earth's water in
rivers and lakes, swamps, and groundwater sources.
There is also water in the air, some appearing as
clouds, and in the cells of living things.

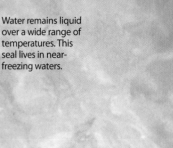

Water remains liquid over a wide range of temperatures. This seal lives in near-freezing waters.

Water flowing over a rocky cliff edge and pounding the rocks below can slowly dissolve minerals in the rock.

ICE ▲

An unusual property of water is that its solid state—ice—floats on top of its liquid state—water, since ice is less dense than water. When water freezes, ice forms from the surface downward. Unlike fish, aquatic mammals such as this Weddell seal must come to the surface to breathe air. This seal has found a breathing hole in the ice.

did you know?..................................

IF EVENLY SPREAD OVER ALL LAND SURFACES, SALT FROM ALL THE OCEANS WOULD FORM A LAYER MORE THAN 500 FEET (152 M) THICK.

WATERFALL ▶

Water is the only natural substance that is found on Earth in all three states: solid, liquid, and gas. Water changes from one state to another in what is called the *hydrologic cycle*. For example, liquid water in lakes, rivers, and oceans evaporates to form water vapor. In the atmosphere, this gas condenses and returns to its liquid state. This constant cycle redistributes water on Earth's surface. Water then shapes the land by dissolving rock and depositing sediments.

WEATHER FRONTS

Air masses are like sumo wrestlers belly bumping in the atmosphere. Suppose a huge body of cold, dry air moves toward a huge body of warm, wet air. The cold air is more dense and slides under the lighter warm air. The warm air rises, cools off, and may form clouds that drop rain. The greater the difference in the temperature and humidity of air masses, the more intense the weather will be when they meet. That's why the boundary between air masses is called a weather *front*, the place where battles take place. Air masses originate in areas called *source regions*. When slow-moving air hangs over these large, mostly uniform stretches of land or water, the air takes on the characteristics of the land below. Dry, or continental, air masses form over land; moist, or maritime, air masses form over oceans. Cold, or polar, air masses form over polar regions; warm, or tropical, air masses, form near the equator.

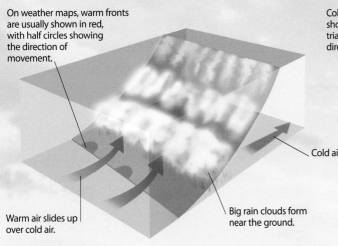

On weather maps, warm fronts are usually shown in red, with half circles showing the direction of movement.

Cold fronts are usually shown in blue, with triangles showing the direction of movement.

Cold air

Warm air slides up over cold air.

Big rain clouds form near the ground.

Fast-moving cold fronts push warm air out of the way.

Warm air rises quickly and condenses into thick storm clouds.

WARM FRONT ▲

The diagram above shows a warm air mass, in red, moving toward a cold air mass, in blue. The leading edge of the warm air mass is a warm front. The warm air is lighter, so it slides slowly up on top of the cold air. Water vapor in the warm air condenses as the air rises and cools, so clouds form. These clouds may dump heavy rain.

COLD FRONT ▲

Above, the blue cold air mass is moving toward the red warm air mass. The cold air is heavy and usually moves faster, pushing the warm air out of the way. If the warm air is also humid, its water vapor may condense and form thunderstorms. Typically, the cold air that passes through after the storms is drier.

did you know? ....
AIR MASSES TYPICALLY COVER HUNDREDS OF THOUSANDS OF SQUARE MILES (MILLIONS OF KM²).

SQUALL LINE: FAST AND FURIOUS ▶

A sudden gusty wind that usually comes with rain is called a *squall*. Squall lines like this one form along fast-moving cold fronts. The row of dark clouds marks the boundary where the cool air mass is pushing up a warm, humid air mass. Until now, this was a good beach day! But severe thunderstorms can form when the warm humid air starts to cool as it rises. Then the bad weather approaches along the advancing front.

GUST FRONT ▶
Unstable atmospheric conditions can have dramatic results. This curved cloud at the edge of a thunderstorm shows the location of a gust front. A gust front is the leading edge of gust winds that are formed by the strong downward currents of air in a thunderstorm. Some gust fronts are strong enough to damage buildings and knock down trees and power lines.

WEIGHTLIFTING

If you said lifting weights is hard work, a physicist would agree. Work is done on an object when the object moves in the same direction in which the force is exerted. Weightlifting involves work that skeletal muscles apply on heavy weights. Weightlifters often do work on one muscle group at a time. Muscles work in pairs and can only contract, or shorten, when they flex. One muscle pulls the bone in one direction. Then the other muscle in the pair pulls the same bone back to its starting position. For example, when you flex the biceps—the muscle on the inside of your upper arm—it contracts, pulling your lower arm upward to your shoulder. To lower the arm again, the triceps muscle on the outside of your upper arm flexes and shortens while the biceps relaxes and lengthens again.

A world-class athlete can push more than 550 pounds (250 kilograms) above the head during a clean and jerk.

In men's competition, the bar alone weighs 44 pounds (20 kg).

COMPETITIVE WEIGHTLIFTING ▶
Competitive weightlifters try to lift as much weight as possible while maintaining good form. To perform a snatch lift, the athlete drops to a squat while lifting the weight above the head and then slowly stands. To perform the clean and jerk, shown here, the athlete lifts the weight from the floor to the chest, and then from the chest to above the head.

The "jerk" part of the clean and jerk involves using the leg muscles to help lift the weight above the head.

The "clean" part of the clean and jerk involves lifting the weight so that the bar rests on the shoulders.

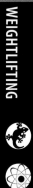

◄ HOW MUCH WEIGHT?

Gyms often set up a series of stations with weights called a *circuit*. The circuit allows you to exercise different groups of muscles. Weights can be free weights, such as barbells, or weight machines where weights are attached to cords. Lifting heavy weights is not recommended for young people who are still growing. Instead, use a weight that you can lift comfortably and that makes your muscles feel tired after a set of 12 to 15 lifts.

A bench press involves lying on your back and pushing a barbell upward to work on pectoralis major, or chest muscles.

A spotter is a coach or training buddy who helps set up your exercise, gives encouragement, and makes sure that you do not get injured.

USING WEIGHTS DURING EXERCISE ▼

Using weights that are light but still provide resistance is called *strength training*. It builds muscle, helps burn calories, and can lead to weight loss. Performing exercises with weights increases the load that the muscles must support. Without a dumbbell or other type of weight, the muscle is supporting only the weight of the limb. When the hand holds a weight, for example, the shoulder muscle's load is increased.

did you know? ....

PULL-UPS, PUSH-UPS, ABDOMINAL CRUNCHES, AND LEG SQUATS INCREASE STRENGTH BECAUSE THEY REQUIRE YOU TO LIFT ALL OR SOME OF YOUR OWN BODY WEIGHT.

This exercise works on the posterior deltoid, a muscle in the back of the shoulder.

The lower back stays straight and almost horizontal.

The knees stay bent to keep the back from becoming rounded.

WHALES

Whales are huge mammals
that have adapted to life in the
water. The blue whale is the
biggest animal living on Earth. The
largest blue whale on record weighed
about 300,000 pounds (about 136,000 kg)
and measured more than 108 feet (about 33 m)
in length. To maintain their huge sizes, whales eat
a lot. The diets of different whale species vary quite a bit.
Some species of whales have teeth—for example, orcas or "killer
whales." They eat different kinds of fish but also hunt seals, sea lions,
and even sharks! Other species, such as the blue and the humpback
whales, have bony plates called *baleen* in the upper jaw. Baleen
whales eat millions of zooplankton and tiny fish every day. They gulp
great amounts of water and strain the food using their baleen. A
whale's body is covered by a thick layer of fat called *blubber,* which can
be up to a foot and a half thick (about 46 cm). Blubber keeps whales
warm in freezing temperatures and, since blubber is lighter than
water, it allows whales to float better.

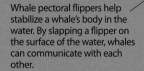

Whale pectoral flippers help
stabilize a whale's body in the
water. By slapping a flipper on
the surface of the water, whales
can communicate with each
other.

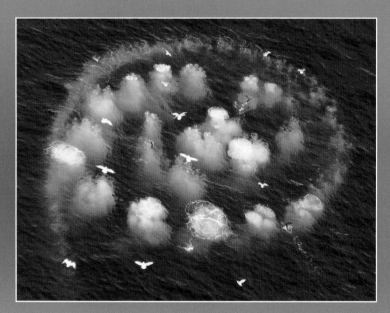

▲ **BUBBLE NETTING**
Some humpback whales cast their own nets when
fishing—only their nets are made of bubbles! A group
of whales dives deep below a school of fish. One whale
blows bubbles while swimming in a circle. The bubbles
rise up and form a cylinder of bubbles that the fish will
not swim through. Then the other whales, with their
mouths open wide, lunge to the surface through the
middle of the cylinder. They get a huge mouthful of
water and fish.

A whale's ears are
very sensitive. Whales
can hear other whale
calls across hundreds
of miles of ocean.

▼ WHALE PODS

Whales are social creatures that live in groups called *pods*. Some group members are old and others are young calves. A whale in a pod may live close to its parents for several years. Groups are especially effective when working together to round up fish with bubble nets, and for protecting the calves from predators. If predators threaten a sperm whale calf, the adults form a ring around the calf, facing outward. To get to the calf, the predator would probably think twice before attempting to get past the massive adults! Whales also produce amazing sounds to communicate with each other in breeding grounds, to hunt schools of fish, and to locate geographic features in the ocean as they migrate. Scientists have shown that whales can hear their calls through hundreds of miles of ocean.

The tail, or fluke, of a whale is very strong. It is used to propel the animal forward. Flukes also allow scientists to identify each animal by its unique tail markings.

SPOUTING ▶

Because they are mammals, whales need to breathe air. They must come to the surface. Whales breathe through blowholes located near the top of their head. Blue whales can hold air in their lungs for more than 30 minutes, and sperm whales can do it for up to 1.5 hours! When the whale exhales or spouts, the moist warm air from its lungs is released into the outside air, forming a cloud. Some spouts can reach a height of 33 feet (10 m).

did you know? BOWHEAD WHALES CAN LIVE CLOSE TO 200 YEARS!

WIND POWER

Concern about the world's increasing demand for energy, a limited supply of fossil fuels, and the effects of burning these fuels has led some people to ask: What renewable energy sources can be used to produce electricity efficiently and inexpensively? One answer is wind power. For centuries, people have designed windmills to grind grain, pump water, and even saw wood. In the 1830s, physicist and chemist Michael Faraday found that mechanical energy could be turned into electricity. This discovery, and the work of other scientists that followed, led to the idea of using wind to power a turbine to produce electricity. The first large-scale wind turbine, built in 1888, produced only 12 kilowatts of electricity. Just one of today's largest commercial wind turbines can produce between 6 and 7 million watts, or megawatts, of electricity—enough to power about 1,800 U.S. homes.

Anemometer, a sensor to measure wind speed

High voltage transformers.

Nacelle side panel

Nacelle

Nacelle bottom panel

◄ HARVESTING THE WIND

Most wind turbines spin at a height of about 262 feet (80 m) above the ground. Scientists calculated wind speeds at that altitude to find locations where the wind is strongest. They measured the strongest winds offshore and along certain coastlines. The turbines shown here are located in one of the areas with the highest winds, near the coast in western Australia. Just twelve turbines provide enough electricity to power at least 10,000 homes each year.

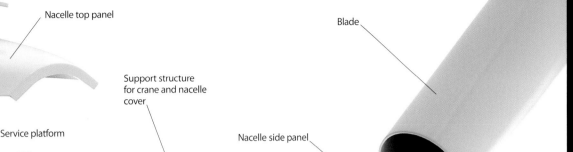

did you know? AS OF 2009, DENMARK GETS 19% OF ITS ELECTRICITY FROM WIND POWER. THIS IS MORE THAN ANY OTHER NATION.

Nacelle top panel

Blade

Support structure for crane and nacelle cover

Service platform

Nacelle side panel

The generator converts the mechanical energy of the spinning blades into electrical energy.

Gearbox

Blades can change angle by swiveling on the hub, which enables the turbine to collect more energy.

The hub cover protects instruments inside.

Motors turn the turbine to face into the wind.

◄ WIND TURBINE

A wind turbine converts the wind's energy into electricity. The wind turns the three blades, which are connected to a hub. All of the turbine's working parts—except for the hub and blades—are contained within an outer casing called the *nacelle*. The nacelle is attached to the top of the tower. Improvements in wind turbine design, such as increased tower height and blade length, have improved wind turbine efficiency and helped reduce the cost of wind energy over the past few decades.

The 3 blades, together with the hub, make up the rotor, in front of the nacelle.

WIND TUNNEL

Suppose you want to test an airplane without actually flying it. Instead of sending the plane through the air, you can send the air around the plane. Wind tunnels allow scientists to model how air flows around vehicles. Scientists use models to test objects or ideas when using the real thing is too expensive, too dangerous, too big, or too small. Wind tunnels are used to better understand aerodynamics—the study of forces that act on objects moving through air. Scientists use wind tunnels to observe the aerodynamics of airplanes, rockets, space shuttles, cars—even people. To do this, they place the study object in a tunnel. Large fans at the end of the tunnel create a strong wind that blows from one end of the tunnel to the other. This wind models the force of air that passes an object when it moves at very high speeds.

AERODYNAMIC TEST ▶

In a wind tunnel, scientists can attach small flags, produce smoke trails, or use laser sensors or cameras to see how air moves around an object at many different points along its surface. Knowing the aerodynamics of a vehicle or its parts can help scientists and engineers perfect its shape and design. They use the data to increase safety, speed, and fuel efficiency.

Increasing or decreasing the wind speed lets the scientist see how the plane might work at different flight speeds.

COMPUTER SIMULATION ▼

Using a computer to model a wind-tunnel test is sometimes cheaper and faster than building a model to test in a wind tunnel. Computer programs can simulate, or imitate, the data collected in a wind tunnel. The colored lines show the layers of air flowing around a virtual plane. Engineers can change the shape of the plane and run the simulation again to perfect the design.

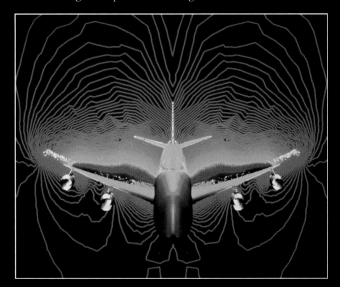

did you know? ....
IN 1901, THE WRIGHT BROTHERS BUILT A WIND TUNNEL TO TEST MORE THAN 200 WING DESIGNS FOR THE WORLD'S FIRST SUCCESSFUL AIRPLANE, WHICH THEY FIRST FLEW IN 1903.

MODELING THE SPACE FLIGHT ▶

Rocket scientists use wind tunnels to model how spacecraft will hold up during launch and reentry into Earth's atmosphere. The small wind tunnel shown here can model motion through air at speeds greater than 1,760 miles per hour (about 2,832 km/h). It can also model airflow high in the atmosphere, where there are many fewer air particles creating pressure than there are near the ground.

Model of space shuttle with liquid booster rocket

Scientists can test different designs of specific airplane parts to see how well they perform in turbulence, or irregular atmospheric motion.

A small-scale model has the exact shape and proportions of the real airplane.

WORKING BODY

The human body operates like a factory in which all the systems must work together to do their jobs. Take a frozen pizza factory, for example. The factory must have an available supply of energy to operate the lights and equipment. Ingredients such as flour, sauce, cheese, and pepperoni must be accessible when the cooks need them. After it comes out of the oven, the pizza has to be frozen and prepared for pickup. Similarly, your body needs energy to perform all its tasks. Your digestive system breaks down food and your circulatory system transports nutrients to your muscular, organ, respiratory, nervous, and other systems. Your brain uses energy to think and tell the rest of your body what to do. When all of your body's systems function properly, you are able to run, breathe, read, eat, and even sleep.

THE BODY'S HARD DRIVE ▲

The brain, like a computer, is a control center and stores information in its memory. It also sends signals to all parts of the body. A computer sends signals by electricity. The brain uses nerves to transmit electrical and chemical messages that tell other systems in the body how to function. The brain is also responsible for learning and recalling information when we need it.

did you know?..

THE LIVER IS LIKE THE FACTORY'S SECURITY SYSTEM: ALMOST EVERY NUTRIENT HAS TO PASS THROUGH IT TO BE TRANSFORMED INTO A MOLECULE THE BODY CAN USE.

▼ CIRCULATION TRANSPORTATION

People depend on cars, subways, and other transportation to get to and from work. Similarly, blood delivers oxygen and nutrients to the cells. Blood picks up carbon dioxide and other wastes from cells and transports them to the excretory, respiratory, and integumentary (skin) systems.

Each worker is hired to perform a specific job, just as each kind of cell is programmed for a certain function. Blood transports cells as well as nutrients and gases. White blood cells fight diseases. Platelets cause clotting to stop bleeding when you cut yourself.

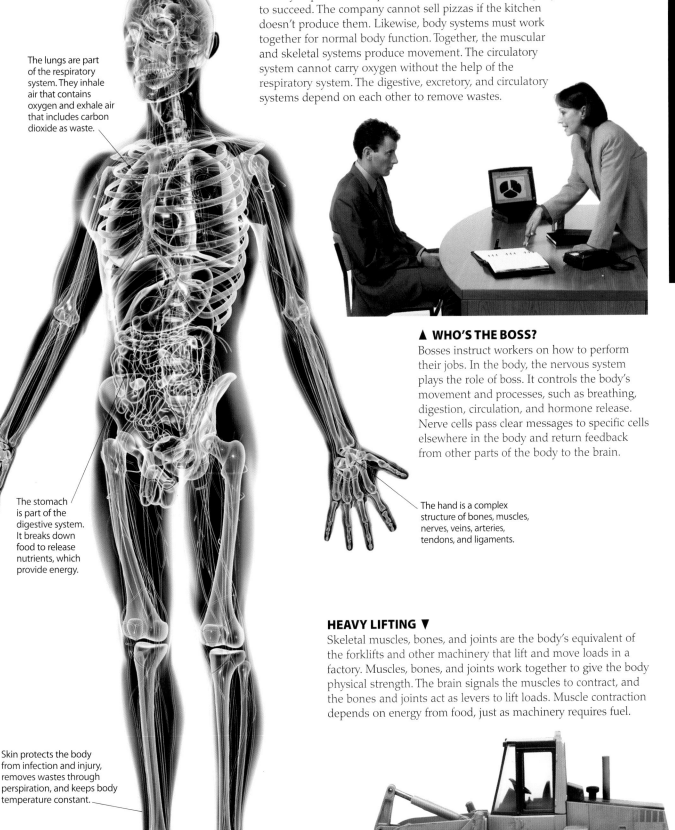

The lungs are part of the respiratory system. They inhale air that contains oxygen and exhale air that includes carbon dioxide as waste.

The stomach is part of the digestive system. It breaks down food to release nutrients, which provide energy.

Skin protects the body from infection and injury, removes wastes through perspiration, and keeps body temperature constant.

The hand is a complex structure of bones, muscles, nerves, veins, arteries, tendons, and ligaments.

◄ TEAMWORK

Factory departments depend on each other for the company to succeed. The company cannot sell pizzas if the kitchen doesn't produce them. Likewise, body systems must work together for normal body function. Together, the muscular and skeletal systems produce movement. The circulatory system cannot carry oxygen without the help of the respiratory system. The digestive, excretory, and circulatory systems depend on each other to remove wastes.

▲ WHO'S THE BOSS?

Bosses instruct workers on how to perform their jobs. In the body, the nervous system plays the role of boss. It controls the body's movement and processes, such as breathing, digestion, circulation, and hormone release. Nerve cells pass clear messages to specific cells elsewhere in the body and return feedback from other parts of the body to the brain.

HEAVY LIFTING ▼

Skeletal muscles, bones, and joints are the body's equivalent of the forklifts and other machinery that lift and move loads in a factory. Muscles, bones, and joints work together to give the body physical strength. The brain signals the muscles to contract, and the bones and joints act as levers to lift loads. Muscle contraction depends on energy from food, just as machinery requires fuel.

WORMS

Worms are also called *annelids*, a name that comes from a Latin word that means "little ring." They are a diverse group of tubelike and ribbonlike animals that have distinctly segmented bodies. Segmented bodies have a lot of advantages. One is the ability to move effectively without limbs, by contracting and relaxing muscles that change the worm's shape from short and fat to long and thin. Another is the ability to grow back damaged or missing segments. Some species even reproduce by breaking into fragments that can grow into new individuals! There are more than 9,000 species of worms, divided into three classes. About two thirds of these are marine worms, which inhabit sandy areas in oceans from tropical to arctic regions. Almost a third are earthworms, and about 300 species are leeches. Many worms continually burrow into the sand or soil. Not only do they aerate, or allow oxygen, into the soil, but they leave waste, called *castings*, that fertilize the soil.

Marine worms use paired, paddlelike legs called *parapodia* to crawl and swim.

The king ragworm can grow close to 3 feet (91 cm) in length and have more than 200 individual segments.

King ragworms have powerful, retractable jaws that can deliver a painful bite.

KING RAGWORM ▲

This impressive creature is called a king ragworm. It is an abundant, predatory polychaete, or marine worm, that fishermen often use as bait. The worm lives in mucus-lined burrows in muddy shoreline sand and areas where fresh and salt water meet. King ragworm reproduction occurs when the temperatures rise in the spring. When king ragworm males are ready to mate, they swarm above female worm burrows and release sperm into the water. This triggers the females to release their eggs, which mix with the sperm and are fertilized. After releasing their sperm or eggs, both the male and female ragworms die.

This thickened band of tissue, called the *clitellum*, is always closer to an earthworm's head than to its tail.

Head

did you know? ....
AUSTRALIA'S GIANT GIPPSLAND EARTHWORM CAN REACH LENGTHS OF ABOUT 10 FEET (ALMOST 3 M) AND IS ALMOST AN INCH (2.5 CM) IN DIAMETER!

If its tail is cut off, an earthworm can grow a new one. But the tail that is left over cannot grow a new head.

Tail

Like all worms, earthworms are covered with setae— tiny bristles that are barely visible. Setae help anchor the worms and aid in movement. As invertebrates, earthworms lack skeletons. They move by contracting their muscular segments.

EARTHWORM REPRODUCTION ▲

Earthworms are hermaphrodites—they have both female and male reproductive organs. But they still require a mate for reproduction. To reproduce, two earthworms join together with their heads facing in opposite directions. They pass sperm to one another and then separate. A wide ring of slime then forms around the clitellum. As the worm moves backwards into its burrow, the ring of slime begins to slide off the worm. As the slime moves, it passes over the deposited sperm and the part of the worm that contains the eggs. The eggs and sperm are released into the slime. When the slime slides off the worm, it dries up, forming a cocoon with the eggs and sperm inside. The earthworms hatch in about 30 to 60 days, but can take years if the conditions are not just right!

EARTHWORM ANATOMY ▶

An earthworm's front end contains the mouth, brain, and major organs, including 5 hearts! These structures function as hearts, but are not actual hearts, so they are called *pseudo-hearts*. Earthworms have a gizzard, where strong muscles and grains of sand enable them to grind up food. The back end of the worm contains intestines and blood vessels. Instead of eyes, ears, or a nose, worms have receptor cells at their tips that sense light and movement. Worms breathe by absorbing oxygen through pores in their skin—a process that works only if the worms are wet.

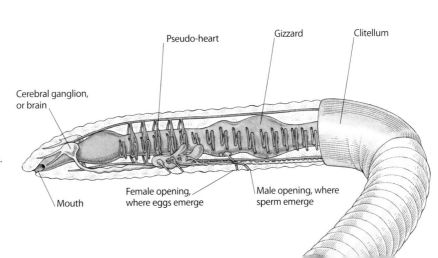

Pseudo-heart

Gizzard

Clitellum

Cerebral ganglion, or brain

Mouth

Female opening, where eggs emerge

Male opening, where sperm emerge

DK EDUCATION

Design Miranda Brown and Ali Scrivens, The Book Makers
Managing Art Editor Richard Czapnik
Design Director Stuart Jackman
Publisher Sophie Mitchell

PEARSON

The people who made up the *DK Big Ideas of Science Reference Library* team—representing digital product development, editorial, editorial services, manufacturing, and production—are listed below.

Johanna Burke, Jessica Chase, Arthur Ciccone, Amanda Ferguson, Kathryn Fobert, Christian Henry, Sharon Inglis, Russ Lappa, Dotti Marshall, Robyn Matzke, Tim McDonald, Maria Milczarek, Célio Pedrosa, Stephanie Rogers, Logan Schmidt, Christine Whitney

CREDITS